LANGENSCHEIDTS MUSTERBRIEFE

100 Briefe Englisch

für Export und Import

Neubearbeitung
von
Birgit Abegg und Michael Benford

LANGENSCHEIDT

BERLIN · MÜNCHEN · LEIPZIG · WIEN · ZÜRICH · NEW YORK

Auflage:	5.	4.	3.	2.	1.	Letzte Zahlen
Jahr:	1998	97	96	95	94	maßgeblich

Druck: Druckhaus Langenscheidt, Berlin-Schöneberg
Printed in Germany

ISBN 3-468-41121-9

Vorwort

„Langenscheidts Musterbriefe“* sind allen, die eine Fremdsprache erlernen, und allen, die Geschäftsbriefe in einer fremden Sprache schreiben müssen, seit Jahrzehnten wohlvertraut. Die in dieser Reihe vorgestellten Musterbriefe haben sich bewährt; man kann sie in der Praxis mit großem Nutzen verwenden.

Die vorliegenden Briefe wurden völlig neu gestaltet und in Inhalt, Stil und Form der heutigen Geschäftspraxis angepaßt. Neben einer selbstverständlich auf den neuesten Stand gebrachten Einweisung in die Form des englischen Geschäftsbriefs werden auch die britischen und amerikanischen Postzustellsysteme und das Telefax behandelt. Weiterhin enthalten die einleitenden Kapitel wichtige Vermerke auf Briefen, Unterschiede zwischen britischem und amerikanischem Englisch sowie Kommentare zu Großschreibung, Silbentrennung und Zeichensetzung.

Den Musterbriefen selbst folgen am Ende einige nützliche Anhänge, einschließlich ein Verzeichnis wichtiger Handelsabkürzungen, und eine Sammlung von Briefmustern und Briefumschlägen im Original-Layout. Ein ausführliches alphabetisches Sachregister am Ende erleichtert den schnellen Zugriff auf den gewünschten Brief oder Begriff.

Die Autoren dieser Neubearbeitung sind Birgit Abegg, staatlich anerkannte Übersetzerin und Gerichtsdolmetscherin, die seit langem in Firmen der deutschen Industrie auch als Dozentin für Wirtschaftssprachen tätig ist, und Michael Benford M. A., der seit vielen Jahren Wirtschaftsenglisch an einer Handelsschule unterrichtet. Beide Autoren sind im Prüfungsausschuß für den Bereich Englisch der Industrie- und Handelskammer zu Düsseldorf tätig.

Autoren und Redaktion möchten sich bei den namentlich genannten Firmen für die erhaltene Unterstützung sowie die Bereitstellung der Originalvorlagen bedanken.

LANGENSCHEIDT

* „Langenscheidts Musterbriefe“ liegen auch für die französische, italienische, spanische und deutsche Sprache vor. Die in den englischen Musterbriefen verzeichneten Namen, Anschriften, Telefon- und Faxnummern sind mit einigen Ausnahmen fingiert. Die darin enthaltenen Warenpreise sind, da sie dauernden Schwankungen unterliegen, nicht als maßgebend anzusehen.

Inhaltsverzeichnis

Die Form des englischen Geschäftsbriefes

Das Layout und die Bestandteile des englischen Geschäftsbriefes unterliegen gewissen Normen und Regeln, die teilweise von denen der deutschen DIN-Normen abweichen.

Die in diesem Zusammenhang relevante britische Publikation ist der "Guide for Typewriting" erarbeitet von der British Standards Institution*. Diese Broschüre vermittelt einen kurzen Einblick in alle Einzelheiten des Layouts und der Form eines Geschäftsbriefes in englischer Sprache. Sie beinhaltet u. a. auch Abkürzungen, Block- oder eingerückte Schreibform, Rechensymbole, die Schreibweise von Zahlen und Brüchen, Zeilenabstände usw.

Im Zeichen des Binnenmarktes und der Annäherung aller Normen innerhalb der EU werden in naher Zukunft sicherlich weitere Anpassungen der internationalen Regeln erfolgen. Dies findet seinen ersten Ausdruck in bereits stattfindenden Sitzungen z.B. einzelner Handelskammern und Verbände, die damit beschäftigt sind, gemeinsame Richtlinien für Prüfungen und Ausbildungsabschlüsse zu verabschieden. Zum heutigen Zeitpunkt kann daher eine endgültige Form, die EU-verbindlich ist, noch nicht gegeben werden.

Die Form englischer Privatbriefe, vor allen Dingen handschriftlich geschriebener, unterliegt in einigen Punkten anderen Gepflogenheiten, Regeln und Normen. Der Langenscheidt-Titel *Dear Jenny... Dear Sir... – Englische Privatbriefe mit deutscher Übersetzung* bietet ausführliche Informationen zu diesem Thema.

Die zur Zeit und im Zuge des Computerzeitalters bevorzugte Form des englischen Geschäftsbriefes besteht aus folgenden Teilen:

1. Briefkopf (letterhead)
2. Bezugszeile (reference line)
3. Datum (date)
4. Anschrift des Empfängers (inside address)
5. Anrede (salutation)
6. Betreff (subject line)
7. Brieftext (body of the letter)
8. Schlußformel (complimentary close)
9. Name und Unterschrift (name and signature)
10. Anlagen (enclosures)
11. Postscriptum (postscript)

Folgender Brief mag als Beispiel für die heute am häufigsten verwendete Form des Geschäftsbriefs dienen:

* British Standards Institution, 2 Park Street, London W1A 2BS.

XYZ Company PO Box 32901 London EC4T 2VC Telephone: 0171 429 5000 Telefax: 0171 320 429	**letterhead**
Your ref: Our ref: JLS/ue	**reference line**
3rd July 19..	**date**
Mr Harald Jaspers Wein- und Spirituosen GmbH Eschbachweg 24 D-40625 Düsseldorf	**inside address**
Dear Mr Jaspers	**salutation**
<u>Your enquiry of 30 June 19..</u>	**subject line**
Thank you very much for your recent enquiry about various gin brands, which we read with great interest. We would be glad to deliver any particular gin you require and are enclosing our latest price list and terms of delivery. Please let us have your detailed enquiry. If you wish to receive any samples, we can send you a trial pack for your convenience. We look forward to hearing from you soon.	**body of the letter**
Yours sincerely	**complimentary close**
John Smith J. L. Smith Sales Manager	**name and signature**
Encs	**enclosures**
P.S. We also enclose information about some of our special discounts.	**postscript**

Die Briefbestandteile

1. Briefkopf (letterhead)

Der Briefkopf ist in der Regel auf dem Briefbogen gedruckt oder er wird bei der Arbeit mit dem Computer in das Schreibprogramm eingespeichert. Der englische Briefkopf muß Namen, Adresse, Telefon- und Telefax-Nummern enthalten. Falls die Firma einen Fernschreibanschluß hat, ist auch dieser anzugeben. Die Namen der Direktoren und die eingetragene Büronummer sind in der Regel ebenfalls zu erwähnen.

2. Bezugszeile (reference line)

Die Bezugszeile besteht gewöhnlich aus den Initialen der Person, die den Brief diktiert hat, und denen der Schreibkraft. Manchmal enthält die Bezugszeile auch ein Geschäftszeichen, das – besonders bei Behörden oder großen Firmen mit zahlreichen Abteilungen – unbedingt in der Antwort angegeben werden sollte.

3. Datum (date)

Die moderne Schreibform für das Datum erlaubt zahlreiche Möglichkeiten, z. B.:

3 July 1993
3rd July 1993
July 3rd 1993
July 3rd, 1993
July 3, 1993

Man sollte mit Rücksicht auf die anders geartete Schreibweise der Amerikaner vermeiden, nur Zahlen zu schreiben, wie z. B.:

1993-7-3

Diese Schreibform für den 3. Juli 1993 wäre in Amerika durchaus üblich, was natürlich zu Verwechslungen führen könnte. Daher sollte der Monatsname ausgeschrieben bzw. vor allem bei längeren Monatsnamen in Kurzform genannt werden, z. B.:

3 Feb 1993

4. Anschrift des Empfängers (inside address)

Beispiele:

Mr J. L. Smith
Mrs A J Gulliver
Ms Jane Mason
Miss Rosemary Thunderbell
Messrs Black & Sons

Einzelpersonen oder Personengesellschaften werden in der Regel mit der oben beschriebenen Weise angeschrieben. “Messrs” steht bei Personengesellschaften nur vor den Namen der Personen, entfällt jedoch, wenn die Personengesellschaft einen Namen hat, der nicht aus Personennamen besteht, z. B.

The British North Sea Oil Company
The Birmingham Polo Club

Adressiert man den Brief an eine Kapitalgesellschaft, die im Englischen z. B. auf “Ltd” bzw. “Plc” endet, im Amerikanischen häufig auf “Inc.”, im Südafrikanischen auf “Pty.” usw., schreibt man lediglich den Namen der Firma, z. B.:

The New York Fire Engine Inc.
Robertson & Partners Ltd
Harward & Freytag Plc

5. Anrede (salutation)

Wie Sie eine Person oder Firma anreden, hängt häufig von der Anrede ab, die Sie bei der Empfängeranschrift verwendet haben. “Mr A J Gulliver” würde man folgendermaßen anreden:

Dear Sir
Dear Mr Gulliver

oder, was im Englischen häufig ist, mit Vornamen:

Dear Adam

Bei Damen gilt ähnliches. “Ms Jane Mason” könnte wie folgt angeredet werden:

Dear Madam
Dear Ms Mason
Dear Jane

Die Abkürzung “Ms” kam ursprünglich aus Amerika, wo Frauen weder ein “Mrs” noch ein “Miss” vor ihren Namen setzen wollten, sondern mit “Ms” lediglich dokumentierten, daß sie weiblichen Geschlechts waren. “Mrs” und “Miss” werden natürlich auch verwendet. Die Abkürzungen “Mr.”, “Mrs.”, “Ms.” werden in amerikanischen Briefen oft mit einem Punkt versehen, in britischen Geschäftsbriefen dagegen nur selten.

Schreibt man an eine Gesellschaft, in der man noch keine Person mit Namen kennt, schreibt man: “Dear Sirs”, “Dear Sir or Madam” oder auch schon “Dear Madam, dear Sir”. In den USA findet immer noch die Anrede “Gentlemen” Verwendung. Falls Zeichensetzung erfolgt, steht nach der Anrede ein Doppelpunkt.

Auf Zeichensetzung wird im Zeitalter des Computers in Anschrift und Anrede bei der Blockform (vgl. Briefmuster S. 155) weitgehend verzichtet. Im Brieftext selbst ist sie natürlich nach wie vor von großer Wichtigkeit. Bei amerikanischen Briefen (vgl. Briefmuster S. 156) ist die Zeichensetzung dagegen oft in Anrede und Schlußformel zu finden. Die für Geschäftsbriefe eher selten verwendete eingerückte Form (vgl. Briefmuster S. 157) verlangt in der Regel die volle Zeichensetzung.

6. Betreff (subject line)

Über die Notwendigkeit eines Betreffs ist man sich innerhalb der verschiedenen Gremien der EU noch nicht einig. Während man in Deutschland offensichtlich noch dazu tendiert, den Betreff als Bestandteil des Briefes aufzufassen, ist er in GB nicht mehr zwingend vorgeschrieben. Obwohl es heißt, daß die Betreffzeile im Englisch nach der der Anrede zu erscheinen hat und nicht vor der Anrede wie im Deutschen, gibt es hiervon auch schon Abweichungen.

7. Brieftext (body of the letter)

Selbst in einem kurzen Geschäftsbrief wird man sich auf drei Teile einigen können: die Einleitung, den eigentlichen Zweck des Briefes und den Schlußsatz.

8. Schlußformel (complimentary close)

Hier gibt es Unterschiede im britischen und amerikanischen Englisch. Während der Brite es sehr genau nimmt, ob er eine Person mit Namen angeredet hat oder nicht, ist der Amerikaner großzügiger.

Schreibt der Brite an eine Person mit Namen, z. B.:

Dear Thomas
Dear Mr Smith

muß er in der Schlußformel "Yours sincerely" schreiben.

Schreibt er allgemein:

Dear Sir
Dear Madam
Dear Sirs

heißt die Schlußformel "Yours faithfully".

Wenn man eine Person recht gut kennt, können einige höfliche Floskeln hinzugefügt werden wie, z. B.:

With best wishes
Kind regards

In den USA findet man häufig:

Sincerely yours, oder
Yours (very) truly

ganz gleich, wie man die Person vorher angeredet hat.

9. Name und Unterschrift (name and signature)

In GB und den USA unterschreibt den Brief in der Regel die Person, die ihn diktiert oder selbst geschrieben hat. Da Unterschriften häufig unleserlich sind, wird es immer gebräuchlicher, den Namen der Person darunterzuschreiben. Um dem Leser die Stellung der Person, mit der er korrespondiert, zu erläutern, steht häufig auch die Berufsbezeichnung unter dem Namen, z. B.:

J L Smith
Sales Manager

Helen Kessler
Personal Assistant

10. Anlagen (enclosures)

Wenn dem Brief eine Anlage hinzugefügt wird, sollte man dies der Ordnung halber am Schluß des Briefes erwähnen. Dies geschieht normalerweise in Form einer Abkürzung, "encl", "enc(s)".

11. Postskriptum (postscript)

Dieses dient wie im Deutschen dazu, noch etwas unter den Brief zu setzen, das man vergessen hat. Es ist jedoch heute recht selten geworden, da in computergeschriebene Briefe unschwer etwas eingefügt werden kann.

Wichtige Behandlungsvermerke auf Briefen

By airmail	per Luftpost
By registered mail	per Einschreiben
By courier	per Kurier
c/o (care of)	per Adresse, bei
attn (for the attention of)	zu Händen von
Express Delivery	Eilboten
If undelivered, please return	falls unzustellbar, bitte zurück
To be forwarded Please forward	Bitte nachsenden
P. O. Box	Post(schließ)fach
Poste restante To be called for	Postlagernd
Printed matter	Drucksache
Printed matter reduced rate	Drucksache zu ermäßigter Gebühr
Urgent	Eilt
Confidential	Vertraulich
Private and confidential	Streng vertraulich
Private	Privat

Adressen – Die britischen und amerikanischen Postzustellsysteme – Die Postleitzahlen

In Großbritannien gibt es noch immer zwei Postzustellsysteme "first class post", etwa Postzustelldienst 1. Klasse, und "second class post", etwa Postzustelldienst 2. Klasse, welcher billiger, aber auch langsamer ist.

Jede Adresse in Großbritannien hat einen "postcode", eine Postleitzahl, die aus jeweils zwei Gruppen von Buchstaben und Zahlen besteht. Die erste Gruppe zeigt an, in welche Stadt oder ihre Umgebung der Adressat postalisch einzuordnen ist. Die 2. Gruppe gibt genauen Aufschluß über die Adresse innerhalb dieses Wohngebiets.

Da Maschinen diese Zahlen- und Buchstabengruppen noch nicht erfassen können, werden sie von Postbediensteten als "blue dots" (blaue Punkte) auf die Umschläge getippt. Diese können von elektronischen Sortiermaschinen mit einer Geschwindigkeit von 16 000 Stück pro Stunde gelesen und sortiert werden.

Eine richtig geschriebene Adresse sollte wie folgt aussehen:

> Ms Anne Howard
> 16 Garden Avenue
> Harwich
> Essex
> C012 4JR
> England

Die Länderbezeichnung ist nur erforderlich, wenn der Brief außerhalb von Großbritannien abgeschickt wird.

Die Namen der wichtigsten postalisch anerkannten Abkürzungen für Grafschaften lauten wie folgt:

Bedfordshire	Beds	Northamptonshire	Northants
Berkshire	Berks	Northumberland	Northd
Buckinghamshire	Bucks	Nottinghamshire	Notts
Cambridgeshire	Cambs	Oxfordshire	Oxon
Gloucestershire	Glos	Shropshire	Shrops/Salop
Hampshire	Hants	South Glamorgan	S Glam
Hertfordshire	Herts	Staffordshire	Staffs
Lancashire	Lancs	West Glamorgan	W Glam
Leicestershire	Leics	Wiltshire	Wilts
Lincolnshire	Lincs	Worcestershire	Worcs
Mid Glamorgan	M Glam	Yorkshire	Yorks
Middlesex	Middx		

Bei der Adressierung ist es in den USA wichtig, die Abkürzung für den jeweiligen Staat in zwei Großbuchstaben sowie die Postleitzahl (die im amerikanischen Englisch "ZIP code" heißt) anzugeben.

In den Vereinigten Staaten ist es üblich, die Adresse in Großbuchstaben und ohne Zeichensetzung auf den Umschlag zu schreiben, z. B.:

MS ANNE SMITH
57 MAIN DRIVE
FLORIDA FL 935281
USA

Die Namen der US-Staaten und deren Gebiete mit Abkürzungen lauten wie folgt:

Alabama	AL	Kansas	KS	Ohio	OH
Alaska	AK	Kentucky	KY	Oklahoma	OK
Arizona	AZ	Louisiana	LA	Oregon	OR
Arkansas	AR	Maine	ME	Pennsylvania	PA
California	CA	Maryland	MD	Puerto Rico	PR
Canal Zone	CZ	Massachusetts	MA	Rhode Island	RI
Colorado	CO	Michigan	MI	South Carolina	SC
Connecticut	CT	Minnesota	MN	South Dakota	SD
Delaware	DE	Mississippi	MS	Tennessee	TN
District of Columbia	DC	Missouri	MO	Texas	TX
Florida	FL	Montana	MT	Utah	UT
Georgia	GA	Nebraska	NE	Vermont	VT
Guam	GU	Nevada	NV	Virginia	VA
Hawaii	HI	New Hampshire	NH	Virgin Islands	VI
Idaho	ID	New Jersey	NJ	Washington	WA
Illinois	IL	New Mexico	NM	West Virginia	WV
Indiana	IN	New York	NY	Wisconsin	WI
Iowa	IA	North Carolina	NC	Wyoming	WY
		North Dakota	ND		

Muster für richtig adressierte Briefumschläge befinden sich auf S. 158.

Das Telefax

In einer Zeit ständig steigender mündlicher Kommunikationsmöglichkeiten und immer schnellerer schriftlicher Nachrichtenübermittlungswege hat sich das Telefax schon heute einen nicht mehr wegzudenkenden Platz erobert und das Fernschreiben weitestgehend verdrängt.

Telefaxe sind geschäftsbriefähnliche, jedoch meist weniger formgebundene schriftliche Nachrichten, die über getrennte Faxgeräte, die telefonisch anwählbar sind, oder auch computergesteuert direkt vom Absender an den Empfänger geschickt werden können.

Die äußere Form eines Telefax unterliegt noch keinen festen Normen. In der Regel werden zumindest Absender und Empfänger und die entsprechenden Fax-Nummern erwähnt, wie z. B.

FAX MESSAGE

From: John Smith on 0171 2804025 (Tel. and Fax)
To: Ms Lydia Haverkamp on 010 49 211 534453

Date: 21 Aug 19..

Dear Lydia

This is to confirm that I sent you the required documents yesterday.

Kindest regards
Yours sincerely

John

John Smith

Weitere Muster für Telefaxe befinden sich z. B. auf den Seiten 21, 72 und 87. Da Telefaxe direkt geschickt werden, wird natürlich kein Briefumschlag benutzt.

Ein Fax gilt im privaten Geschäftsverkehr als hundertprozentig rechtsverbindlich, da es den vollen Beweis für die Abgabe einer Willenserklärung erbringt. Davon zu unterscheiden ist der Behörden- und Gerichtsbereich, in dem es zum größten Teil als rechtswirksam, auch für die Einhaltung von Fristen, gilt. Hier ist aber Vorsicht geboten, da die Rechtsprechung noch nicht als endgültig anzusehen ist. In den USA hingegen wird das Fax mit Bestätigungsvermerk bereits hundertprozentig von den Behörden anerkannt.

Britisches und amerikanisches Englisch

Die Unterschiede zwischen britischem und amerikanischem Englisch, die für die schriftliche Geschäftskommunikation relevant sind, sind nicht so ausgeprägt wie in der Umgangssprache oder in anderen Bereichen. Detaillierte Auskunft hierüber gibt ein gutes einsprachiges Wörterbuch, wie z.B. das *Dictionary of English Language and Culture*, Longman, 1992. Zwei Aspekte sind aber für das Schreiben von Briefen im allgemeinen wichtig, nämlich die Unterschiede in der Rechtschreibung und im Wortschatz.

Rechtschreibung

Gegenüber dem britischen Englisch (BE) weist die Rechtschreibung im amerikanischen Englisch (AE) hauptsächlich folgende Eigenheiten auf:

1. Häufige Weglassung des Bindestrichs, z.B. *newsstand, breakdown, soapbox, cooperate.* Viele dieser Weglassungen finden zunehmend im BE Verbreitung.
2. Viele Wörter, die im BE auf **-our** enden, enden im amerikanischen Englisch auf **-or**, z.B. *color, humor, favor, honorable.*
3. Viele Wörter, die im BE auf **-re** enden, enden im AE auf **-er**, z.B. theater, center, fiber. Ausnahme: *massacre*.
4. Viele Wörter, die im BE auf **-gue** enden, lassen das **-ue** im AE weg, z.B.: *catalog, dialog.*
5. Viele Wörter, die im BE auf **-ce** enden, enden im AE auf **-se**, z.B.: *license, defense, practise* (im AE auch im Substantiv).
6. Wortstämme, die im BE auf **-l** enden, verdoppeln dieses, wenn die Endsilbe mit einem Vokal beginnt. Im AE entfällt das zweite **-l**, z.B.: *dial* – BE *dialled*, AE *dialed, travel* – BE *travelled*, AE *traveled.*
7. Stummes **-e-** entfällt im AE in Wörtern wie *abridg(e)ment, judg(e)ment, acknowledg(e)ment.*
8. Neben *although, all right, through* finden sich die informell-familiären Formen *altho, alright, thru.*
9. Weitere Unterschiede in der Schreibweise gibt es bei Wörtern, wie z.B.

BE	**AE**
tyre	tire
cheque	check
aluminium	aluminum

Wortschatz

Im Laufe der Zeit haben sich in den USA vom BE abweichende Bezeichnungen durchgesetzt, wie z. B.:

BE	AE
autumn	fall
underground, tube	subway
motorway	highway, freeway
queue	line
petrol (station)	gas (station)
flyover	overpass
flat	apartment, condo
ground floor	first floor
first floor	second floor
lift	elevator
pavement	sidewalk
rates	property tax
timetable	schedule
toilet	bathroom, restroom
company	corporation
public limited company	stock corporation

Silbentrennung

Im Gegensatz zum Deutschen werden englische Wörter nicht immer streng nach Silben getrennt, es gilt aber schon der Grundsatz, daß nur zwei- oder mehrsilbige Wörter überhaupt getrennt werden dürfen. Wörter wie z.B. "asked" oder "called" werden nicht getrennt.

Im allgemeinen hat das Prinzip der Erkennbarkeit des jeweiligen Wortes oder Wortteils Vorrang, um dem Leser zu ermöglichen, das Wort richtig auszusprechen. Das Wort "listen" kann z.B. nur zwischen "s" und "t" getrennt werden: "lis-ten", weil eine Trennung hinter dem "t" den Leser dazu verleiten würde, das Wort falsch mit hörbarem "t" auszusprechen, d. h. "list-" gefolgt von "-en". Ähnliche Beispiele sind "co-inci-dence" (nicht "coin-cidence") und "coin-age" (nicht "co-inage"). Ein weiteres Beispiel wäre auch "ˈphoto-graph" und "pho-ˈtogra-pher". Wörter mit gleicher Schreibung aber anderer Lautung wie "(a) ˈpresent" und "(to) preˈsent" müssen auch entsprechend der Regel der Erkennbarkeit getrennt werden, und zwar "(a) ˈpres-ent" und "(to) pre-ˈsent".

Des weiteren ist es normalerweise nicht zulässig, ein Wort so zu trennen, daß nur zwei Buchstaben am Anfang der zweiten Zeile erscheinen (z.B. vor der "-ed" Endung). Zwei Buchstaben am Ende der ersten Zeile sind zwar möglich (z.B. re-produce), aber nicht wünschenswert.

Vorsilben wie "ante-" oder "anti-" werden nicht getrennt. Doppelbuchstaben werden getrennt (z.B. al-low, dis-solve, con-nect, as-sume, in-nocu-ous), es sei denn, daß eine Trennung die Bestandteile des Wortes irreführend darstellt (z.B. inn-keeper, call-ing, pass-ing).

Interpunktion

Das Apostroph

Ein Apostroph kann besitzanzeigend gebraucht werden: "The Manager's car is outside", "The managers' cars are outside.", oder es ersetzt einen fehlenden Buchstaben: "The Manager's here." (d.h. "The Manager is here.").

In seltenen Fällen kann die Mehrzahl mit Apostroph-s gebildet werden, und zwar bei Zahlen: "the 70's and the 80's" (wobei die Schreibweise ohne Apostroph als akzeptabel gilt: "the 70s and the 80s"), oder bei Wörtern, die normalerweise keine Mehrzahl besitzen: "too many if's and but's".

Das Komma

Abweichend vom Deutschen ist das Komma nur in seltenen Fällen ein streng vorgeschriebenes Satzzeichen. Nebensätze werden nicht immer vom Hauptsatz durch ein Komma getrennt, und zwar vor allem nicht bei Objektsätzen (z.B. "He knows that I'm English."). Bei "if"-Sätzen wird bei kürzeren Sätzen das Komma oft weggelassen, bei längeren Sätzen dagegen zur besseren Überschaubarkeit gesetzt:

> Call me if he comes.
>
> If the Managing Director asks me to contact him, I'd like you to leave a message with my secretary.

Ein Komma symbolisiert oft eine Sprechpause. Demzufolge erscheint es dort, wo der Sprecher kurz innehalten würde, z. B. vor und nach "however", "nevertheless", "strangely enough" usw.

Kommas werden benutzt, um einen nicht notwendigen Relativsatz vom Hauptsatz zu trennen: "My brother John, who lives in London, is here." Notwendige Relativsätze werden vom Hauptsatz nicht durch Kommas getrennt: "The man who came yesterday is here again."

Groß- und Kleinschreibung

In englischen Geschäftsbriefen gelten die sonst üblichen Regeln der Groß- und Kleinschreibung der englischen Sprache, aber zur Hervorhebung wichtiger Wörter in der Handelskorrespondenz, wie z.B. Bill of Lading, Certificate of Origin, Commercial Invoice usw., können große Anfangsbuchstaben verwendet werden.

Wenn auf die Titel von Mitarbeitern einer Firma, die bestimmte Positionen innehaben, Bezug genommen wird, ist ein großer Anfangsbuchstabe erforderlich: "The Manager has instructed the Finance Controller to redraft the Commercial Invoice."

Einfache Anfrage
Simple enquiry

1

25 November 19..

Clearcut Lawnmowers Ltd
90–100 Clover Drive
TORRINGTON
Kent
TZ3 8ZZ
United Kingdom

Dear Sirs

We are a newly-established firm specializing in the supply of gardening equipment. As we are currently in the process of buying in stock in good time for the coming spring season, we would be grateful if you would send us a catalogue of your full lawnmower range, both mechanical and electric.

Would you also indicate how much time should be allowed for delivery and include details of your export prices and quantity discounts. Please also state whether goods on a sale or return basis can be supplied and what your position on after-sales service is.

If your products are to good standard and delivery is prompt, we feel sure that there will be ample opportunity for your company to acquire a substantial share of the market here.

Yours faithfully
Brill Gartengeräte GmbH

Thomas Wolf
Assistant Manager

newly-established neugegründet
gardening equipment Gartengerät
buy in stock Lagervorräte einkaufen
lawnmower Rasenmäher
range Serie, Palette
export price Exportpreis
quantity discount Mengenrabatt
sale or return Kauf mit Rückgaberecht
after-sales service Kundendienst
be to good standard einem guten Standard entsprechen
ample opportunity reichlich Gelegenheit
share of the market Marktanteil

2 Anfrage
Enquiry

February 28, 19..

Computronic Inc
PO Box 8732
Austin, TX 75110
USA

Gentlemen:

ENCRYPTION SOFTWARE

We read your advertisement in the latest edition of DataNews, in which you state that you have developed new software for the encryption of electronic data.

We are in the process of reviewing our company's security procedures and wish to introduce a hierarchical system of data access using unbreakable passwords.

We would be most interested in receiving a demonstration version of your encryption program, which we would then attempt to crack. If, using a powerful mainframe computer, we do not succeed, we will place a substantial order for your software.

We look forward to receiving your comments on this matter, together with details of on-site after-sales service and up-date facilities, should you feel that your product will pass the test we intend it to undergo.

Yours truly,
BOCHUMER DATENTECHNIK

Reinhardt Deutsch
Software Engineer

encryption Verschlüsselung, Kodierung
electronic data elektronische Daten
security procedure Sicherheitsverfahren
data access Datenzugang
unbreakable passwords unaufschlüsselbare Kennwörter
demonstration version Vorführversion
crack knacken
mainframe computer Großrechner
comments Stellungnahme
on-site an Ort und Stelle
after-sales service Kundendienst
up-date auf den neuesten Stand bringen

Anfrage auf Grund eines Tenders
Enquiry based on a tender

TELEFAX

23 March 19..

TO: POLISH CHAMBER OF COMMERCE
FAX: 010 4822 274673

FROM: BILL JAMBOR, Lancashire Enterprises plc
FAX: 01773 721029

Dear Sirs

My company is at present tendering for an EC project in Romania. I would be pleased if you could send me details of Polish companies able to supply the following equipment:

1. Engine compressor spare parts, engine spare parts and pistons for Ikarus motor vehicles, Types 260.50, 280.33, 280.64
2. Spare parts for "Tatra" Trams, type T4R
3. Electrolyte copper cathode and 18mm diameter copper winding wire
4. Equipment and spare parts for diesel electric and electric locomotives
5. Rail coach batteries, locomotive starter batteries and locomotive storage batteries

The exact details and conditions of tender will be sent to the relevant companies.

We unfortunately have very little time to submit our tender and would thus be grateful to receive details from you as soon as possible and in any event in no later than two weeks from now.

Yours faithfully
...

tender (formell) anbieten, sich an einer Ausschreibung beteiligen
compressor Kompressor
engine spare part Maschinenersatzteil
piston Kolben
electrolyte Elektrolyt
copper cathode Kupferkathode
winding wire Wickeldraht
rail coach battery Eisenbahnwaggonbatterie
starter battery Starterbatterie
storage battery Speicherbatterie
submit unterbreiten

4 Anfrage auf Grund einer Anzeige
Enquiry in response to an advertisement

22 March 19..

Liberty Damenmoden GmbH
Viktoriastr. 99
47166 Duisburg
Germany

For the attention of Monika Prinzen

Dear Ms Prinzen

LADIES' SUMMER WEAR

We refer to your advertisement in the this month's edition of "Fashion Plus".

We are a major importer of ladies' fashion wear with a network of retail outlets throughout the UK. For the past 10 years we have, with considerable success, been dealing in fashions for teenagers and the early 20s. Our lines are strictly up-market and are always in instant response to current trends.

Please send us your catalogue, a current export price-list including terms of payment and delivery and details of quantity discounts. We would also appreciate it if you would include representative samples of some of this season's garments to enable us to assess their quality.

We feel sure that there could be considerable openings for competitively priced goods of the right design and look forward to hearing from you in good time for the coming season.

Yours sincerely
CHELSEA FASHION LTD
...

major importer größerer Importeur
retail outlet Einzelhandelsverkaufsstelle
the early 20s Leute Anfang 20
line *hier:* Stil, Kollektion
be strictly up-market *hier:* den höchsten Ansprüchen genügen
be in instant response *hier:* sofort reagieren
current trend aktueller Trend
export price-list Exportpreisliste
quantity discount Mengenrabatt
openings *hier:* Chancen, Möglichkeiten
competitively priced goods Waren zu konkurrenzfähigen Preisen

Unverlangtes Angebot
Unsolicited offer

Lancashire Enterprises plc
Enterprise House
17 Ribblesdale Place
Winckley Square
Preston PR7 3NA

Genesis Medical Ltd
115 Gloucester Road
London S.W.7

12 December 19..

Dear Sirs

SINGLE USE TRANSFUSION SET

We were given your name by our mutual business associate, Neil Smith at Medical Systems (International) Ltd, who recommended that we contact you.

Lancashire Enterprises plc is actively involved in eastern Europe, having won major contracts to help revitalise the industrial base of countries effecting the transition to a market economy. Included in this work is the provision of a trading service.

In this respect we have been approached by a Polish manufacturer of Single Use Transfusion Sets (sample enclosed), who has requested us to seek business contacts in western Europe on his behalf.

As sole UK agents for the manufacturer, we are able to supply you the sets at a CIF unit price of £ .... We are able to supply 8500 units per shipment and up to three shipments per month.

The manufacturing process used conforms to international standards. The manufacturer is in the process of applying for the Department of Health certificate and would welcome an order subject to obtaining such certification.

.../2

single use transfusion set Einwegbesteck für Transfusionen
business associate Geschäftspartner
win major contracts den Zuschlag für größere Aufträge erhalten
revitalise wiederbeleben
effect the transition to den Übergang zu ... verwirklichen
market economy Marktwirtschaft
provision *hier:* Bereitstellung
seek business contacts Geschäftskontakte suchen
sole agent Alleinvertreter
manufacturing process Herstellungsverfahren
international standards internationale Normen

2/

In addition, if a good response from UK firms is forthcoming, the packaging will be modified and the instructions will be printed in English.

Furthermore, should you so require, the product can be modified to suit individual requirements.

We look forward to your response and would welcome an opportunity to strengthen ties with eastern Europe. We also enclose for your information a brochure describing our activities in this field in more detail.

Yours faithfully
Lancashire Enterprises plc

Bill Jambor
Project Executive

Enc

Department of Health
(brit.) Gesundheitsministerium
subject to
sofern, ... unter der Bedingung, daß
be forthcoming
sich einstellen, erfolgen
suit individual requirements
individuellen Bedürfnissen entsprechen
strengthen ties with
Bindungen mit ... stärken

Unverlangtes Angebot
Unsolicited offer

6

June 19..

Schulz Import- und Export
Handelsgesellschaft mbH
Kurfürstenstr. 20
90459 Nürnberg
GERMANY

Gentlemen:

Subject: Door-to-Door Delivery

Don't throw this letter away! It's worth real money to anybody who'll give us a chance to prove just how good we are!

Why worry about keeping to those delivery dates stipulated in your Sales Contract using the regular, state-owned mail service when you can make use of a custom-made personalized, door-to-door delivery service right now! We have a fleet of trucks near your town and, likely as not, based near your block, just waiting to rush your goods to their destinations.

We have already made ourselves into a household name in the US and now, by popular request, we have extended our operation to Europe, East and West. We can provide transportation for anything from a string of pearls to a pipeline – to any destination you care to name. Just call us on a local low-toll number and we'll quote you right away. We specialize in rock-bottom priced, just-in-time delivery with full insurance cover.

We're waiting to hear from you. Just pick up that phone and call us – you'll never look back!

Sincerely yours,
...

stipulate festsetzen
state-owned mail service staatliches Postzustellungssystem
custom-made nach Kundenangaben erstellt
door-to-door delivery service Zustelldienst von Haus zu Haus
fleet of trucks Lkw-Fuhrpark
household name bekannter Name
string of pearls Perlenschnur
low-toll number Nummer zu niedriger (Fernsprech) Gebühr
rock-bottom price niedrigst kalkulierter Preis
full insurance cover volle Versicherungsdeckung

7 Verlangtes Angebot
Solicited offer

May 21, 19..

Ex- und Import Industriegüter
Handelsgesellschaft mbH
Kernerplatz 4
70182 Stuttgart
GERMANY

Attn. Mr. Rolf Stein

Dear Mr. Stein,

Many thanks for your enquiry of May 10 regarding the importation of our new, environmentally friendly, CFC-free packaging material.

We will have no difficulty in manufacturing and supplying the shapes you describe in the drawings included with your enquiry, since we have a molding technique which enables us to customize packaging to customers' specifications. So far, we have had an overwhelming response from all over the world to our new product and our production department is being expanded to cope with the increasing demand.

We enclose our catalog and current export pricelist. All prices are exclusive of tax and are quoted FCA US airport. At present, delivery to a US airport can be made within 3–4 weeks of receipt of order. We look forward to executing your order and enclose our Order Form for customer convenience.

Truly yours,
...

environmentally friendly umweltfreundlich
CFC-free = chlorofluorocarbon-free FCKW-frei = frei von Fluorchlorkohlenwasserstoffen
packaging material Verpackungsmaterial
molding technique Formtechnik
customize auf den Kundenbedarf zuschneiden
catalog Katalog
exclusive of tax ohne Steuer
FCA = Free Carrier *(Incoterm)*
order form Auftragsformular
for customer convenience für die Bequemlichkeit des Kunden

Beschwerde über unzulängliche Waren
Complaint about imperfect goods

8

7 December 19..

Turnpike Traders Ltd
Units 1–4
Greenman Industrial Estate
Blackburn
Lancashire
BB1 5QF

Dear Sirs

This morning we took delivery of the 50 boards of prime quality teak ordered as per our letter of 1 November (Order No. WW-T1-11).

The quality of 2 of the boards is, however, unsatisfactory as they contain large, unsightly knots rendering them unsuitable for use.

We feel sure that this is an oversight on your part but, owing to the considerable number of orders in hand, we had no alternative but to return the goods in question to you, carriage forward, on the assumption that you will arrange for replacements to be sent to us by return to enable us to keep to production schedules.

We trust that you will be in agreement with this course of action and look forward to receiving replacements corresponding to your otherwise high standards.

Yours faithfully
WELLING & BURBURY LIMITED

William Welling
Chief Executive

prime quality teak erstklassiges Teakholz
unsatisfactory nicht zufriedenstellend
unsightly unansehnlich, häßlich
unsuitable for use unbenutzbar
oversight Versehen
order in hand vorliegender Auftrag
carriage forward unfrei, Fracht vom Empfänger zu zahlen
by return umgehend
keep to *hier:* einhalten
production schedule Produktionsplan
be in agreement with einverstanden sein mit
high standard hohes Niveau, gute Qualität

9 Berichtigung einer Reklamation
Adjustment of a claim

March 26, 19..

Magnetische Informations- und Datensysteme
Gewerbepark
59069 Hamm
GERMANY

Attn: Mr. Andreas Schulz

Dear Mr. Schulz:

Subject: Complaint re DRT/398 Semi-conductors

Thank you for your communication of March 10, in which you state that the semi-conductors supplied are not up to standard.

Having looked into the matter we are now able to tell you that you were mistakenly supplied with DRT/298 semi-conductors, which, despite having similar properties to the latest version, are not able to perform as consistently as their successor.

We apologize for the inconvenience caused and would suggest that we either take back the consignment, carriage forward with insurance covered by us and replace it by DRT/398s, or reduce the price of the goods you have received to the standard list-price, with a further discount of 10% to make up for the inconvenience caused.

Please fax us your reply at your earliest convenience. Should you opt for a replacement delivery we will rush the goods to you by airmail.

Sincerely yours,
...

semiconductor Halbleiter
be up to standard dem (normalen) Standard entsprechen
look into the matter die Sache untersuchen
be mistakenly supplied fälschlicherweise beliefert werden
similar property ähnliche Eigenschaft
consistently gleichmäßig, zuverlässig
inconvenience Unannehmlichkeit
with insurance covered by us Versicherungsdeckung durch uns
make up for entschädigen für
opt for sich entscheiden für
replacement delivery Ersatzlieferung

Bitte um Bankauskunft
Application for a bank reference

10

15 February 19..

Benson Bank plc
42 Leadenhall Street
London EC1 7HJ

Dear Sir or Madam

A. P. Jones & Sons Limited
Account Number 28625309

The above-mentioned customer has approached us requesting a credit facility amounting to £15,000 per month on 30-day terms.

We would be most grateful if you would advise us whether the company in question is sufficiently sound for such a facility.

Should you so prefer, please feel free to reply via our bankers, SouthWest plc, Hounslow Bath Road Branch, Middlesex MX1 4WW quoting our account number 29560277.

Any information given will, of course, be treated in the strictest confidence with no obligation on your part.

Yours faithfully
INTERFORM LTD

P. J. Smith
Managing Director

approach s.o. sich an j-n wenden
credit facility Kreditmöglichkeit, Kreditbetrag
on 30-day terms mit 30tägiger Laufzeit
advise *hier:* mitteilen
sufficiently ausreichend
sound solide, gesund
via über, durch
our bankers unsere Bank(verbindung)
account number Kontonummer
in the strictest confidence streng vertraulich
with no obligation on your part für Sie unverbindlich

11 Negative Bankauskunft
Unfavourable bank reference

28 February 19..

Charles Cape & Co Ltd
42 New Fetter Lane
London EC1A 4WW

Dear Sirs

Easifit Car Accessories Limited

In response to your request for a reference regarding the above-mentioned firm, we must point out that the firm in question has not been known to us for long.

We are thus unable to furnish you with the information you require.

We regret not being in a position to assist you in this matter.

Yours faithfully
NorthEast Bank plc

T. B. Smith
Assistant Manager
Corporate Accounts Dept.

accessory
Zubehör(teil)
in response to
als Antwort auf
point out
hinweisen auf
firm in question
fragliche Firma
furnish s.o. with s. th.
j-n mit etw. beliefern, j-m etw. geben
be in a position
in der Lage sein
Corporate Accounts Dept.
Abteilung für Geschäftskunden

Neutrale Bankauskunft

Non-committal bank reference

12

March 31, 19..

IGI Gesellschaft für Handel,
Export und Import
Schwanallee 135
35037 Marburg
Germany

STRICTLY CONFIDENTIAL

Gentlemen:

Thank you for enquiry regarding the company you refer to in your letter of March 15.

Due to the fact that we have only held the subject's account for some six months now we are not able to assist you in this matter.

We regret not being able to help you this time.

Sincerely yours,

Thomas G. Slade
Business Accounts Division

due to the fact that auf Grund der Tatsache, daß
hold an account ein Konto führen
subject *hier:* Kunde, Firma
assist helfen
Business Accounts Division Geschäftskonten-abteilung, Abteilung für Geschäftskunden

13 Bitte um Kreditauskunft
Request for a credit reference

➡ Brief 14

Funke-Kaiser GmbH
Nordstraße 24
47169 Duisburg
Germany

U2/45
23 July 19..

Hamlyn Engineering
Golden Crescent
Hayes
Middlesex MX1 UB3
England

PRIVATE AND CONFIDENTIAL

Dear Sirs

We have recently been approached by the firm mentioned on the enclosed slip, who have requested us to grant them a credit facility amounting to £5,000 per quarter. We understand from the firm in question that you have been dealing with them for some time and they have suggested that we request you to supply an appropriate trade reference.

We would be grateful if you would kindly reply to the following questions to enable us to conclude whether the business of subject is sufficiently sound to support the facility mentioned. Your early response using the stamped addressed envelope enclosed would be much appreciated.

1. How long has subject been known to you?
2. What amount of credit facility do you normally allow subject?
3. On what terms do you trade with subject?

.../2

private and confidential streng vertraulich
slip Blatt, Zettel
credit facility Kreditrahmen
per quarter vierteljährlich
appropriate geeignet, angemessen
trade reference Handelsauskunft
business of subject *hier:* die in Frage stehende Firma
sound solide, gesund
support *hier:* verdienen
addressed envelope adressierter Umschlag
subject *hier:* die betreffende Firma

2/

4. Are payments made promptly / slowly / very slowly?
5. Have you ever had occasion to threaten to take legal proceedings to recover sums due to you?
6. Please also give any other information you feel is relevant.

We assure you that any information given will be treated in the strictest confidence. Please do not hesitate to contact us in future should you require us to reciprocate.

Yours faithfully
FUNKE-KAISER GmbH

Johannes Schmitt
Managing Director

Enc

take legal proceedings
gerichtliche Schritte unternehmen
recover sums
Summen eintreiben
due to s. o.
fällig an j-n
relevant
wichtig, bedeutend
treat behandeln
reciprocate
hier: einen Gegendienst erweisen

14 Positive Kreditauskunft einer Firma
Favourable credit reference from a firm

➡ Brief 13

30 July 19..

Funke-Kaiser GmbH
Nordstraße 24
47169 Duisburg
Germany

CONFIDENTIAL

Dear Mr. Schmitt

In response to your letter dated 23 July 19.., ref. No. U2/45, we are pleased to supply you with the following information.

The firm in question are well established on the local market and have a good reputation. As far as we know they have been trading for over 15 years in our field of enterprise and have built up a sizeable network of overseas customers.

We have been dealing with them for the past 8 years now on quarterly account terms and are pleased to report that they have always met their financial commitments punctually and in full. We have, thus far, extended them a credit line of up to £2,500 in any given quarter but would have no hesitation in increasing it to double this figure, should the need arise.

We trust that this information will be of use to you and would point out that it is given in the strictest confidence with no obligation whatsoever on our part.

Yours sincerely
HAMLYN ENGINEERING

Harry Hamlyn
Chief Executive

field of enterprise Unternehmensbereich
sizeable (ziemlich) groß, beträchtlich
overseas *(von GB aus):* ausländisch *sonst:* überseeisch
on quarterly account terms mit vierteljährlichem Zahlungsziel
meet one's financial commitments seinen finanziellen Verpflichtungen nachkommen
extend *hier:* gewähren
credit line Kreditlinie
in any given quarter in jedem beliebigen Quartal
on our part unsererseits

Informationen für einen potentiellen Kunden
Information for a prospective customer

15

28 April 19..

Coupre Links 401
9000 GENT
Belgium

Fax: 010 32 56 773058

Dear Sir or Madam

RE: SOURCING GINSENG ROOTS

With reference to our fax of 22 April please note that our contacts in China have just confirmed that small samples and descriptive literature have been despatched. As soon as we receive this material we will pass it on to you.

The price CIF Antwerp is generally something in the region of US$ 25 per kg - types, quality, minimum order quantity, delivery etc. to be confirmed.

In the meantime we would appreciate some information on your company's background and financial standing. We would point out at this juncture that it is to be expected that the Chinese supplier will stipulate payment by letter of credit.

Should you have any queries please do not hesitate to contact us.

Yours faithfully
Lancashire Enterprises plc

Mannix Fu
Project Executive / Trade Dept.

source Bezugsquelle finden
root Wurzel
sample Muster
descriptive literature Informationsmaterial
despatch schicken, (ver)senden
be something in the region of sich etwa bewegen um
minimum order quantity Mindestbestellmenge
financial standing finanzielle Lage
at this juncture an dieser Stelle, in diesem Augenblick
stipulate festsetzen
payment by letter of credit Zahlung per Akkreditiv
trade dept Handelsabtlg.

16 Postwurfsendung / Rundschreiben
Mail shot / circular

18 February 19..

Prince DIY Centre
75 – 95 New Hall Street
Oxford OX1 7HH

Dear Customer

DIY ON YOUR DOORSTEP!

We are delighted to report that customer demand for our unbeaten range of "do-it-yourself" equipment and materials has increased at such a staggering pace, that we are shortly to be opening a second branch just outside town on the new Pricewise Trading Estate.

Our new branch, at 42–50 Grove Road, will provide ample parking facilities and will stock all the lines you have come to know and rely on together with a whole new range of modestly priced accessories for the DIY-enthusiast working on his own. This range will include "one-hand" tools enabling the handiman (or woman!) to manipulate equipment with one hand only, leaving the other free.

Just to convince you how serious we are, we're offering a 5% discount on all cash sales over £25 during the first month of business as from the first of next month. We'll deliver all bulky items (marked with a red star on the price tag) to your front door absolutely free of charge within a 25-mile radius.

So don't miss the chance of cashing in on our once-in-a-lifetime throw-away offers! We're looking forward to greeting you on our new premises on June 1st and we're absolutely certain you'll be glad you came!

Yours faithfully
...

at a staggering pace in einem schwindelerregenden Tempo
parking facilities Parkmöglichkeiten
modestly priced accessories Zubehörteile zu bescheidenen Preisen
"one-hand" tool Werkzeug, das mit einer Hand bedient werden kann
handiman *hier:* Heimwerker
cash sale Barverkauf
bulky groß, sperrig
price tag Preisschild
within a 25-mile radius in einem Umkreis von 25 Meilen
miss the chance die Gelegenheit verpassen
once-in-a-lifetime einmal im Leben vorkommend
a throw-away offer *hier:* ein einmalig preiswertes Angebot

Ausstellung eines unwiderruflichen Dokumentenakkreditivs
Issue of an irrevocable documentary credit

17

12 September 19..

Torrington Marine Co Ltd
Unit 8
Greenway Industrial Estate
Blackburn
BA3 8IJ
Lancashire

Dear Sirs

We have been requested by the Bank of International Commerce in the Sultanate of Oman to advise the issue of their irrevocable Credit Number 344912/92 in your favour for account of

MidEast Marine

of Kuwi, Sultanate of Oman, P.O. Box 61842, for £25,000 (SAY TWENTY-FIVE THOUSAND POUNDS STERLING) available by your drafts on us at 30 days sight accompanied by the following documents:

1. Signed invoices in triplicate certifying goods are in accordance with order No. 2092/92 dated 15 August 19.. between MidEast Marine and Torrington Marine Co Ltd.

2. Marine and War Risk Insurance Certificate covering "All risks" warehouse to warehouse, for 10% above the CIF value, evidencing that claims are payable in the Sultanate of Oman.

3. Complete set 3/3 Shipping Company's clean "on board" ocean Bills of Lading made out to order of the shippers and endorsed to order of the Bank of International Commerce, Sultanate of Oman,

.../2

for account of
auf Rechnung von
draft on us
auf uns gezogener Wechsel
at 30 days sight
auf 30 Tage Sicht
in triplicate
dreifach
marine and war risk insurance certificate
Versicherungszertifikat zur Abdeckung des See- und Kriegsrisikos
all risks
alle Risiken
clean "on board" ocean bill of lading
reines "an Bord" Seekonnossement
make out to order
an Order ausstellen
endorse
indossieren
freight paid
Fracht bezahlt

2/

marked "Freight Paid" and "Notify MidEast Marine of Kuwi, Sultanate of Oman, P.O. Box 61842".

Covering: 3x Type 500-D Outboard Motors CIF Muscat
Shipped from UK Port to Muscat
Partshipment prohibited
Transhipment prohibited
Documents must be presented for payment within 15 days from the date of shipment.

We are requested to add our confirmation to this Credit and we hereby undertake to pay you the face amount of your drafts drawn within its terms, provided such drafts bear the number and date of the Credit and that the Letter of Credit and all amendments thereto are attached.

The Credit is subject to Uniform Customs and Practices for Documentary Credits (1983 Revision), International Chamber of Commerce Publication No. 400.

Drafts shown under this Credit must be presented to us for payment / negotiation / acceptance not later than 12 October 19.. and marked "Drawn under Credit Number 344912/92" of the Bank of International Commerce Sultanate of Oman.

Dated ...

Signed ...

p.p.
York Bank plc
91 Mosley Street
Manchester MA1 3UZ

outboard motor
Außenbordmotor
partshipment
Teilverschiffung
transhipment
Umladung
undertake
sich verpflichten
face amount
Nennwert
amendment
Änderung
attach
beifügen
be subject to
unterliegen
uniform
einheitlich
negotiation
hier: Begebung
acceptance
Akzept

Vergabe eines bestimmten Auftrages
Placing a specific order

18

➡ Briefe 19–22

17 October 19..

Lupton Bros Ltd
P.O. Box 8
Fountain Works
Portland Street
Accrington
Lancashire
BB5 1RJ
England

Dear Sirs

OUR PURCHASE ORDER NO.5769F/KED

We refer to your fax No. 0254 36279 dated 5 October 19.. relating to our enquiry No. 921/KED and wish to place an order for the following items:

QTY.	DESCRIPTION	U. PRICE	T. PRICE
5,000	Rubberized spindles for Northrop looms	£0.80	£4,000.00
	Khedival mail line (agency)		£40.00
	Legalization and certification		£150.00
	TOTAL PRICE FOB		£4,190.00

(SAY FOUR THOUSAND ONE HUNDRED AND NINETY POUNDS STERLING ONLY)

purchase order Kauforder
place an order einen Auftrag erteilen
item Position
qty = quantity Menge
description Beschreibung
u. = unit price Einheitspreis
t. = total price Gesamtpreis
rubberized spindle gummierte Spindel
loom Webstuhl, Webmaschine
legalization Beglaubigung
certification Bescheinigung

TERMS

PRICES	The above prices are firm and subject to no future change and are quoted FOB, packing included.
	N.B. Kindly let us have a new Pro-forma Invoice in 10 (ten) copies, showing FOB prices, fixed delivery period and terms of payment.
PAYMENT	Against a confirmed L/C only. Should any extension of the validity of the credit be necessary as a result of your being at fault, extra expenses incurred will be charged to you.
	N.B. This order is subject to the approval of the appropriate Egyptian authorities and to the opening of the necessary credit in your favour.
DELIVERY	4 months from opening of L/C.
INSURANCE & FREIGHT	As per our circulars enclosed.
CONDITIONS OF SHIPMENT	Shipment by container is not allowed. Shipment to be effected through: KHEDIVAL MAIL LINE (AGENCY) AIRWORK HOUSE 35 PICCADILLY L O N D O N

We look forward to receiving your confirmation and remain

Yours faithfully
SOCIÉTÉ MISR DE FILATURE
ET DE TISSAGE FIN
...

firm fest
be subject to unterliegen
packing included einschließlich Verpackung
pro-forma invoice Proforma-Rechnung
fixed delivery period feste Lieferzeit
term of payment Zahlungsbedingung
confirmed L/C bestätigtes Akkreditiv
extension Verlängerung
validity Gültigkeit
be at fault im Verzug sein, auch: im Unrecht sein
extra expenses Zusatzkosten
incur auftreten
shipment Verschiffung
confirmation Bestätigung

Auftragsbestätigung
Confirmation of Order

19

➡ Briefe 18, 20 – 22

1 November 19..

Your ref.: 5769F/KED
Our ref.: GE/tt

Société Misr de Filature
et de Tissage Fin
KAFR EL DAWAR A.R.E.
EGYPT

Dear Sirs

Thank you for your letter of 17 October.

We hereby confirm your Purchase Order No. 5769 F/KED for 5,000 rubberized spindles for Northrop looms, total price £4,190.00, FOB U.K. port, payment to be made by confirmed L/C.

We note your Conditions of Shipment and confirm that the order will be effected as per the provisions of your Insurance and Freight Circulars.

As requested we enclose a new pro-forma invoice and ten copies thereof.

We trust the goods will arrive punctually and in good condition and look forward to doing further business with you in the future.

Yours faithfully
LUPTON BROS LTD

G. Etherington
Export Manager

Encs

rubberized spindle gummierte Spindel
loom Webstuhl, Webmaschine
confirmed L/C bestätigtes Akkreditiv
note *hier:* feststellen, zur Kenntnis nehmen
effect ausführen
as per gemäß
provision Vorkehrung, Bestimmung
Insurance and Freight Circular Versicherungs- und Fracht-Rundbrief
trust glauben, vertrauen

20 Versicherungs- und Verschiffungsanweisungen, Verzollung
Insurance and shipping instructions, customs clearance

➡ Briefe 18, 19, 21, 22

Société Misr de Filature
et de Tissage Fin
KAFR EL DAWAR A.R.E.
EGYPT

INSURANCE AND FREIGHT CIRCULAR

Dear Sirs

Further to our attached order we wish to draw your attention to our Insurance & Shipping Instructions and would point out that they are also those observed by ourselves.

1. SHIPPING METHOD
(a) Goods must be transported in the hold of the ship.
(b) Shipping to be effected using ships not more than 20 years old and also according to the Institute of London Underwriters classification clause.

2. SHIPPING INSTRUCTIONS
All cases should be marked S.M. followed by the number of the case, followed by the total number of cases in the consignment.

Example: If the cases are part of order 8706 and the total number of cases in the consignment amounts to 4, the cases should be marked:

S.M./8706/1/4 S.M./8706/2/4 S.M./8706/3/4
S.M./8706/4/4

When despatching the order please airmail us the NAME of the SHIP on which the goods are to be shipped and the number of the purchase order relating to the consignment. This information will be of great assistance to us in tracing the goods upon their arrival at port and in proceeding with their clearance through customs immediately, thus avoiding delay.

attached beigefügt
shipping method Art der Verschiffung
hold Laderaum (eines Schiffes)
cargo-bearing ship die Ladung beförderndes Schiff
effect shipping Verschiffung durchführen
according to entsprechend, gemäß
classification clause Klassifizierungs-, Bewertungsklausel
Underwriter Versicherer
consignment Sendung
despatch versenden
purchase order Kauforder
be of assistance hilfreich sein
trace *hier:* finden
proceed with *hier:* durchführen, erledigen
clearance through customs Zollabfertigung

3. DETAILS TO BE COMMUNICATED TO US
Please arrange for us to receive, at least 24 hours before sailing date, details of the consignment together with the following information to enable us to effect the required insurance:
(a) Name of the carrying ship
(b) Value of the goods despatched
(c) Port of loading

Before shipping any consignment, the value of which amounts to or exceeds E£30,000 (thirty thousand Egyptian pounds) at any one time, the above information must be communicated to us

TELEGRAPHICALLY

For ordinary orders the information, as specified above, can be sent by AIRMAIL letter.
N.B. Failure to communicate details to us telegraphically, as specified above, will oblige us to hold you responsible for any decision prejudicial to ourselves in connection with our open insurance policy.

4. FREIGHT
"From port of despatch to Alexandria port", to be payable at destination, in "EGYPTIAN CURRENCY".

5. CLEARANCE
To enable us to clear the goods through customs please airmail us the appropriate invoice, packing and specification lists in 10 (ten) copies or more if possible.

In this respect we would draw your attention to the fact that by sending your invoices and packing lists etc. as requested you will save us a considerable amount of time and will, above all, avoid complications with our customs authorities.

Please follow the above instructions for all consignments sent against our orders. We depend on your co-operation for us to receive the information required in good time.

Yours faithfully
...

sailing date Abfahrtsdatum (bei Schiffen)
port of loading (Auf-)Ladehafen
amount to sich belaufen auf
exceed übersteigen
failure Unterlassung
oblige s.o. j-n zwingen, verpflichten
hold s.o. responsible j-n verantwortlich machen
prejudicial schädlich
open insurance policy Generalversicherungspolice
port of despatch Versandhafen
destination Bestimmungsort
currency Währung
clearance *hier:* Verzollung
invoice Rechnung
packing list Packliste
customs authorities Zollbehörden
depend on abhängen von
co-operation Mitarbeit
in good time rechtzeitig

21 Versandanzeige (Versandavis)
Advice of Despatch

➡ Briefe 18–20, 22

Lupton Bros Ltd
P.O. Box 8
Accrington
Lancashire BB5 1RJ
England

1 January 19..

Your ref.: 5769F/KED
Our ref.: GE/tt

Société Misr de Filature
et de Tissage Fin
KAFR EL DAWAR A.R.E.
EGYPT

Dear Sirs

Your Purchase Order No. 5769F/KED

We are pleased to inform you that the goods ordered as per the above mentioned purchase order have been despatched in accordance with your instructions.

They have been packed in 5 cases, 100 to a case. The cases are marked S.M./5769F/KED and numbered 1-5/5.

The consignment is being shipped on board m.v. "Egyptian Star", which is due to leave Southampton at the end of this month, arriving in Alexandria on 15 March.

We have handed our sight draft for £4,190.00 to the Arabian Bank, London together with the documents required under the terms of the L/C, namely: a complete set of clean, shipped on board Bs/L

.../2

purchase order Kauforder
in accordance with in Übereinstimmung mit
100 to a case 100 pro Kiste
on board a vessel an Bord eines Schiffes
m.v. *Abkürzung für:* **motor vessel** Motorschiff
sight draft Sichtwechsel
L/C *Abkürzung für:* **letter of credit** Akkreditiv
complete set vollständiger Satz
clean B/L reines Konnossement

2/

endorsed to your order, marked in accordance with your specifications; one original and ten copies of the commercial invoice; a certificate of U.K. origin duly legalized by the Arab Republic of Egypt Representation; a declaration from the Egyptian Company for Maritime Transport "Martrans", evidencing that the goods have been shipped by them; a packing list; insurance certificate in triplicate.

The Arabian Bank has paid the sum.

We trust that the goods will be to your complete satisfaction and look forward to hearing from you again. We also enclose for your information some changes to our current price list.

Yours faithfully
LUPTON BROS LTD

G. Etherington
Export Manager

Enc

endorse
indossieren
commercial invoice
Handelsfaktura
certificate of origin
Ursprungszeugnis
duly legalized
vorschriftsmäßig beglaubigt
maritime transport
Seetransport
evidence
beweisen
packing list
Packliste
insurance certificate
Versicherungszertifikat
in triplicate
in 3facher Ausfertigung
be to one's complete satisfaction
zu j-s vollster Zufriedenheit ausfallen

22 Beschwerde - Reklamation
Complaint

➡ Briefe 18–21

20 March 19..

Lupton Bros Ltd
P.O. Box 8
Accrington
Lancashire BB5 1RJ
ENGLAND

Dear Sirs

Our Purchase Order No. 5769F/KED

With reference to the above-mentioned order for 5,000 rubberized spindles we regret to advise you that checks have revealed that the rubber at the base of approx. 40% of the spindles is in an unsatisfactory condition. It would appear that the rubber is perished owing to storage in strong sunlight or as a result of having been left outside for a prolonged period of time. We have airmailed you a sample spindle under separate cover for you to inspect yourselves.

You will appreciate that we are unable to install the defective parts in our looms and are therefore forced to run our mill at reduced capacity. This, in turn, has caused delays in delivery for our clients, who, should the delay continue, will have no alternative but to seek an alternative source of supply.

We therefore need 2,000 replacements in perfect condition immediately and would suggest that you despatch them to us by air freight, carriage paid.

We feel obliged to point out that your handling of this matter will determine whether we will be able to continue our business relationship in future.

Yours faithfully
SOCIÉTÉ MISR DE FILATURE
ET DE TISSAGE FIN
...

rubberized spindle gummierte Spindel
reveal (auf)zeigen
to be perished spröde sein
storage Lagerung
in strong sunlight in starkem Sonnenlicht
prolonged verlängert
appreciate *hier:* verstehen
install einbauen
loom Webstuhl, Webmaschine
mill Fabrik
source of supply Lieferquelle
replacement Ersatz
by air freight per Luftfracht
carriage paid Fracht bezahlt
handling Behandlung

Versandanzeige
Advice of Despatch

10 May 19..

MacGraw Landfill Inc.
PO box 25376
St. Louis, MO 63178
USA

Gentlemen:

As per your Order No. 231/ZH of April 30 we have despatched a VX 78 tire-shredder to you using InterTrans as freight forwarders. They, in turn, advise us that the machine will be shipped on board m.v. "Ariadne" which is due to leave Rotterdam on May 15 and will dock in Norfolk, Virginia at the end of June.

Under the FCA terms agreed the machine will be placed at your disposal at InterTrans's depot in St. Louis by June 30 at the latest.

Sincerely yours,
KREFELD MASCHINENBAU GmbH

Günther Willmann
Export Manager

tire shredder Reifen-Shredder
freight forwarder Frachtspediteur
in turn ihrerseits
m.v. = motor vessel Motorschiff
be due to leave fällig zur Abfahrt sein
dock ins Dock gehen
depot Depot, Lagerhaus

24 Ankündigung einer Qualitätskontrolle
Notification of a quality control examination

Stahlexport GmbH
Taunusstr. 12-14
46119 Oberhausen
Germany

2nd May 19..

Dear Mr Meier

<u>Our Order 19345692 TI</u>

Thank you for your telex of April 25 in which you state that the steel plates will be ready for dispatch and awaiting shipment in a fortnight's time.

In our L/C we stipulate that we require a commercial invoice, the B/L and the insurance certificate for shipment CIF Bangkok together with a quality control report. As regards this latter we have entrusted the company we name below with quality control and they will be contacting you in the next few days. They are:

SGS
Société Générale de Surveillance
German Office Hamburg

Would you please enclose this company's assessment with the documentation to be presented to both the issuing and the advising banks.

Thank you in advance for your help.

Yours sincerely
SOUTH EAST ASIA STEEL
...

steel plate Stahlplatte
await shipment zum Versand, zur Verschiffung bereitstehen
L/C = letter of credit Akkreditiv
commercial invoice Handelsfaktura
B/L = bill of lading Konnossement
insurance certificate Versicherungszertifikat
quality control report Qualitätskontrollbericht
entrust beauftragen, anvertrauen
assessment *hier:* Bericht
documentation Dokumentation, Papiere
issuing bank eröffnende Bank *(beim Akkreditiv)*
advising bank avisierende Bank *(beim Akkreditiv)*

Bitte um Übersendung einer Proforma-Rechnung
Request for pro-forma invoice

25

10 April 19..

Diamantsägen Wilde GmbH
Ritterstraße 9
31785 Hamburg
GERMANY

Dear Mr Wilde

Our Enquiry PL/384 of 2nd March 19..
Your Offer No. 58391 of 21st March 19..

We are pleased to inform you that your DX 33 saw-blades wholly conform to our quality requirements. We should therefore like to place an order for 25 units, provided you can see your way clear to granting us a further rebate of 5% on your prices as quoted in the above-mentioned offer. We feel that the volume of the order we are interested in placing would justify this small concession.

However, to enable us to import these saw-blades into India we will need to apply for an import licence from our local Government authorities and would therefore ask you to send us a pro-forma invoice to include the following details:

- exact description of the goods
- unit and total price with discounts
- terms of payments and delivery CIF Calcutta
- packing list

We would be grateful if you would send the pro-forma invoice by registered mail. As soon as we have received the import licence, we shall telex our order to you and open the L/C with our bankers.

Yours sincerely
...

saw-blade Sägeblatt
conform to entsprechen
unit Einheit, Stück
grant gewähren
rebate Nachlaß
volume of the order Auftragsvolumen
justify rechtfertigen
import licence Importlizenz
authority Behörde
pro-forma invoice Proforma-Rechnung
packing list Packliste
by registered mail per Einschreiben
open the L/C das Akkreditiv eröffnen

26 Übersendung der Rechnung
Sending the invoice

Your ref: Fm/ly
Our ref: SM/52/ip

7 January 19..

Mr Arthur M Jones
Laser Engineering Ltd
1 Victoria Square
Birmingham B1 1BD
UNITED KINGDOM

Dear Mr Jones

Your Order 835/XI of 15 Dec 19..

We are pleased to inform you that the articles, as per the above-mentioned order, were despatched by lorry yesterday. They will be shipped across the Channel on board SS Marina tomorrow and are due to arrive at your premises at the beginning of next week.

Please find enclosed our invoice No. 351 685 T for DM 17,850.00 including all transport costs. We would ask you to settle it either by bank transfer or by cheque within 30 days, subject to the usual early payment discount of 3 per cent.

We trust that you will receive the goods in perfect condition and remain at your service for further deliveries at any time.

Yours sincerely
Daffur & Sattel GmbH

Hans Broich
Export Dept.

by lorry per LKW
the Channel der Ärmelkanal
premises Geschäfts-, Büroräume
transport costs Transportkosten
settle *hier:* bezahlen
by bank transfer per Banküberweisung
by cheque per Scheck
the usual early payment discount der für sofortige (baldige) Zahlung übliche Nachlaß
further deliveries weitere Lieferungen

Bitte um offenes Zahlungsziel
Request for open account terms

27

November 25, 19..

Seaboard Industries plc
Grand Avenue
Hove
East Sussex BN3 2LS
Great Britain

Gentlemen:

As you know, we have been customers of your company for almost two years now and have always settled our invoices punctually by letter of credit in the pre-agreed way.

This is why we feel that we can now request you to grant us payment on open account terms for further deliveries, viz a 3-month payment period against presentation of your quarterly statement.

We feel that we have now earned this short-term credit facility, particularly because we aim to be placing further and possibly more substantial orders with you in the near future.

Awaiting your news with interest,

Yours very truly,
Marting & Campals Inc.

Christopher P. Jefferson
Assistant Manager

settle an invoice eine Rechnung begleichen
letter of credit Akkreditiv
in the pre-agreed way in der vorher abgesprochenen Art und Weise
viz nämlich, das heißt
a 3-month payment period ein 3monatiges Zahlungsziel
presentation Vorlage
quarterly statement vierteljährlicher Kontoauszug
short-term credit facility kurzfristige Kreditmöglichkeit
more substantial orders größere Aufträge

28 Kundenkonto: Klärung einer Unstimmigkeit
Customer's account: clarification of a discrepancy

12 July 19..

Ms Maria de Lurdes Fontes Pereira
Fontes & Melo Ltda.
Rua de D. Afonso Henriques, 49
P-1300 Lisboa
PORTUGAL

Dear Ms Pereira

Balancing of Our Quarterly Account
to June 30th 19..

We confirm the receipt of your quarterly account showing a debit balance for us of £475.50.

After comparing your statement with our figures, however, we find that there is a discrepancy. According to our records our debit balance only amounts to £375.50. We have checked our invoices thoroughly and have been unable to find any irregularities in our payments. Could it be that your figure is a misprint?

We have of today advised our Invoicing Department to remit the equivalent of £375.50 in Portuguese Escudos to your account by bank transfer and would request you to check your figures once again. Should you arrive at a figure differing from ours, please let us know, specifying the exact nature of the difference of £100.00, for which we ourselves have no explanation.

We hope that this matter can be solved quickly and without any further inconvenience. For your information we are sending you enclosed a copy of our own statement.

Yours sincerely
...

quarterly vierteljährlich
debit balance Sollsaldo
statement Kontoauszug
discrepancy Unstimmigkeit
record Eintragung
thoroughly sorgfältig
irregularity Unregelmäßigkeit, Unstimmigkeit
Invoicing Department Rechnungsabteilung
remit überweisen
equivalent Gegenwert
arrive at a figure auf eine Zahl kommen
differ sich unterscheiden

Detailliertes Angebot von Reiseweckern
Detailed offer for travelling alarm clocks

29

The Clock Company Ltd
Addison Avenue
St. Albans
Herts SA3 1AD

25 September 19..

Patel Trading Co Ltd
Units 4-8 Industrial Estate
Blackburn
Lancs NL3 4 WW

Dear Mr Patel

"Pocket Travelite" Alarm Clock

Our representative in the north of England informs us that you are in the market for electronic travelling alarm clocks. We are pleased to tell you that our latest model, the "Pocket Travelite", has just been launched and will most certainly suit your customers' requirements as regards price, quality, size and performance.

Our company has now been operating in this field for more than five years and in this time we have conducted in-depth market research into customer expectations. Our new "Pocket Travelite" has been tailor-made to correspond to the findings of our customer surveys and we have every confidence in its success. The new model's specifications are as follows:

Casing:	durable and shock-resistant matt plastic case in black, white or burgundy
Battery:	1.5 V, lasts one year on average
Size:	5 cm x 5cm x 3cm
Weight:	150 g

.../2

representative Vertreter
be in the market for vertreiben, verkaufen wollen
launch herausbringen, auf den Markt bringen
performance Leistung
operate *hier:* tätig sein
conduct führen
in-depth gründlich
market research Marktforschung
tailor-made maßgeschneidert
finding Ergebnis
survey (Markt-)Studie
confidence Zuversicht, Vertrauen
durable haltbar
shock-resistant stoßsicher

2/

Features: illuminable digital display; snooze/repeat function; alarm tone increases in volume
Guarantee: 12 months

Servicing: Free, except in cases of misuse, throughout guarantee period
Price: £12.00 per unit

Should you opt to place an initial order for over 100 units we will be pleased to grant you a discount of 10% on the price quoted.

We enclose a sample clock for your inspection together with the full sales literature. Our conditions of sale and delivery are as is customary in the trade and are set out in detail in our brochure.

We look forward to your comments on our offer.

Yours sincerely
THE CLOCK COMPANY Ltd

A.P.T. Smith
Sales Manager

Encs

illuminable beleuchtbar
digital display Digitalanzeige
alarm tone Wecktonstärke
servicing Kundendienst
misuse Mißbrauch
guarantee period Garantiezeitraum
unit Einheit
opt sich entscheiden
initial order Erstauftrag
sample clock Probewecker
sales literature Werbematerial
customary üblich, gebräuchlich
comments Stellungnahme

Rückfrage vor Unterbreitung eines Angebots

Query before submitting an offer

30

9 April 19..

TEG GmbH
Castroper Hellweg 49
44805 Bochum
Germany

Attention: Herr Dix

Dear Mr Dix

Many thanks for your enquiry of March 20 in which you request us to quote prices, terms and delivery dates for our automatic mains-failure petrol-driven electricity generators.

Before submitting you an offer, however, we would be most grateful if you would provide us with a little more information as regards your exact requirements.

1. What voltage do you wish the generators to produce – 220-240 V or 380 V heavy-duty industrial power?

2. How many operating hours should the generators be able to run for before being refuelled?

3. Where will the generators be located? This is important as far as noise level and insulation are concerned. Our range includes both indoor and outdoor models.

We include our catalogue with this letter to give you an overview of our products and would be pleased to quote you on your exact requirements as soon as we have received the information requested.

Yours sincerely
...

mains-failure petrol-driven electricity generator mit Benzin angetriebenes Notstromaggregat
voltage Spannung
heavy-duty industrial power Hochleistungsindustriestrom, Starkstrom
operating hour Betriebsstunde
be refuelled wieder aufgetankt werden
be located angebracht werden
noise level Lärmpegel
insulation Isolierung
range Serie, Palette
overview Überblick

31 Annahme des Auftrags
Accepting an Order

Aw/wc
19 June 19..

Glas Strack
Ruhrallee 95–99
44139 Dortmund
GERMANY

Dear Sirs

Order No. LSG/50/93

We hereby confirm your order for laminated security glass as per your fax of 18 June.

We enclose our pro forma invoice as requested and would ask you to notify us as soon as the L/C has been opened. We will then be able to complete your order within a fortnight of receiving confirmation of the documentary credit from our bankers.

We look forward to hearing from you soon.

Yours faithfully
COOK'S GLASS AND GLAZING

Andrew Warmington
Export Manager

laminated security glass Schichtsicherheitsglas
as per gemäß
pro forma invoice Proforma-Rechnung
notify benachrichtigen
L/C = letter of credit Akkreditiv
complete vervollständigen
within a fortnight innerhalb von 14 Tagen
confirmation Bestätigung
documentary credit Dokumentenakkreditiv

Auftragvergabe an Spediteur für eine Verschiffung
Placing a shipping order with a freight forwarder

32

TD/TT
4 July 19..

INTRASHIP LTD
Eastern Dock
Dover DV9 6QY
ENGLAND

Dear Mrs Horrocks

In the course of this week you will be receiving, FOB Dover, 2 containers of electric guitars and amplifiers marked S.W./93 1-2. They are to be shipped on the first available vessel to Rock Nouveau, 16 rue du Général Leclerc, Bayonne, France. Insurance will be covered by us.

Please make out the B/L to order in triplicate and send all three copies to ourselves. Please also notify us of the name of the vessel as soon as this is known to you.

Yours sincerely
MUSIC AND MORE LTD

Timothy Dearing
Sales Director

electric guitar elektrische Gitarre
amplifier Verstärker
available verfügbar
vessel Schiff
cover (ab)decken
make out ausstellen
B/L = bill of lading Konnossement
to order an Order
in triplicate dreifach
notify benachrichtigen

33 Anfrage nach Frachtsätzen
Enquiry about freight rates

➡ Briefe 34, 35

PW/tt
10 November 19..

Specialised Shipping Services
Unit 20
Coppull Trading Estate
Chorley
Lancs PR7 5AY

Dear Sirs

Please quote us your most favourable freight rates for the transport of 50 tonnes of palletised house bricks, net weight 1 tonne per unit, for shipment from Southampton to Tunis in the first two weeks of December.

Please quote us assuming delivery F.O.B. Southampton stating details of shipping commission and any further charges.

Yours faithfully
WHALEYS BRICKS LTD

Peter Whaley
Production Manager

quote anbieten
favourable günstig
freight rate Frachtsatz
palletise palettisieren, auf Paletten packen
brick Ziegelstein
unit Einheit, Stück
assume annehmen, voraussetzen
detail Einzelheit
commission Provision
further charges weitere Kosten

Frachtangebot
Freight Offer

34

➡ Briefe 33, 35

TT/si
15 November 19..

Whaleys Bricks Ltd
28 Mulberry Road
Winchester
WI3 2WW

Dear Mr Whaley

Your Freight Enquiry of 10 November 19..

Thank you for your enquiry regarding the transport of 50 tonnes of palletised house bricks. Our offer is as follows:

> M.V. CLEETHORPES at £50 per metric tonne or 10 cubic metres, at steamer's option, with 4 lay days

As can be seen from the enclosed sailing card, the vessel is currently located in Marseille and is due to dock in Southampton on November 31st. Loading will commence as from December 1st with an additional charge of £250 for every day of demurrage.

If you accept this offer please forward us the charter party in quadruplicate to enable us to issue the necessary instructions to the ship's captain, Mr Terry Wrigglesworth.

We look forward to your early reply.

Yours sincerely

Theresa Templeton
Specialised Shipping Services

freight enquiry Frachtanfrage
at steamer's option nach Wahl des Dampfers *(gemeint ist hier die Reederei)*
lay day Liegetag
sailing card Schiffsfahrplan
currently zur Zeit
dock ins Dock fahren
load (auf)laden
commence beginnen
as from ab
additional charge zusätzliche Gebühr
demurrage Überliegezeit
forward schicken
charter party Charterpartie
in quadruplicate vierfach

35 Annahme des Frachtangebots
Acceptance of freight offer

➡ Briefe 33, 34

TW/tt
21 November 19..

Specialised Shipping Services
Unit 20
Coppull Trading Estate
Chorley
Lancs PR7 5AY

Fax: 00 44 1524 55057

Dear Ms Templeton

Thank you for your freight offer for palletised house bricks dated 15 November, which we are pleased to accept as follows:

> M.V. CLEETHORPES at £50 per metric tonne or 10 cubic metres, at steamer's option, with 4 lay days

The consignment of house bricks is from Redland Cement Ltd, Unit 10, Greenfields Industrial Estate, Reading and will be delivered F.O.B Southampton by Gotruck Haulage Ltd on December 1st.

You will be receiving the charter party in quadruplicate by separate post in the course of this week.

We hope that there will be no reason for delay of any sort and look forward to our order being shipped as agreed.

Yours sincerely
WHALEYS BRICKS LTD

Terry Whaley
Managing Director

palletised house bricks
auf Paletten gepackte Hausziegel
consignment
Sendung
Industrial Estate
Industriegelände, Gewerbegebiet
by separate post
mit getrennter Post
delay
Verzögerung
of any sort
irgendeiner Art

Einforderung eines Seeversicherungsschadens
Insurance claim after sea-damage

36

15 June 19..

Lion Assurance Ltd
42 Leadenhall St
London EC1 3ZZ

Dear Sirs

We have just taken delivery of a consignment of 200 bales of raw silk which was insured by yourselves. The merchandise was shipped on S.S. Anastasia, which docked in Plymouth on June 10. When our agents inspected the load they discovered that 15 of the bales were spoiled as a consequence of a storm in the South China Sea (survey report included).

We are therefore placing a claim for the damaged goods with you, the details of which are as follows:

Sea-damage 15 bales	
raw silk £1,000 per bale	£15,000.00
Additional expenses	£48.00
Total	£15,048.00

Please arrange to have this sum transferred to our account with the Bergmann Bank in Düsseldorf.

We include all documentation related to this consignment as follows:

1. Insurance certificate
2. Survey report
3. Freight forwarder's invoice
4. Copy of the B/L
5. Ship broker's refusal to grant our claim

We trust you will be able to settle the matter swiftly.

Yours faithfully
...

consignment Sendung
bale Ballen
raw silk Rohseide
merchandise Ware
load Ladung
survey report Gutachterbericht
place a claim eine Forderung anmelden
sea-damage Seeschaden
arrange veranlassen
documentation Unterlagen
be related with zusammenhängen mit
insurance certificate Versicherungszertifikat
freight forwarder Frachtspediteur
B/L = bill of lading Konnossement
ship broker Schiffsmakler

37 Warenanalyse
Analysis of goods

➡ Brief 38

21 October 19..

Cornwall Plastics Ltd
49 Torrington Road
Penzance
PE3 9IK
Cornwall

Dear Sirs

4,200 KG POLYETHERESTER OF SILICIC ACID

We have duly examined the above mentioned consignment and are pleased to submit our "Clean Report of Findings" to you as follows:

Goods submitted for inspection:	4,200 kg polyester of silicic acid as per pro-forma invoice No. 91900252 dated 1 October 19..
Seller:	Cornwall Plastics Ltd Penzance PE3 9IK, Cornwall, UK
Importer:	Slumberland Foam Inc. 92 Fence Rail Road Pittsburgh Pennsylvania PA49721 USA
FOB value:	US$ 19,812.00
CFR value:	US$ 20,412.00
Country of supply:	Great Britain
Quantity:	20
Packing:	drums
Gross weight:	4,543.00 kg
Net weight:	4,200.00 kg
Marks:	CP/PSA92/1-20

silicic acid
Kieselsäure
polyetherester
Polyätherester
consignment
Sendung
report of findings
Untersuchungsbericht
submit
vorlegen
pro-forma invoice
Proforma-Rechnung
gross weight
Bruttogewicht
net weight
Nettogewicht
mark
Markierung

FINDINGS

1. Quality: The quality of the goods submitted to us for inspection has been found to comply with the documents presented to us inasmuch as their examination is within our mandate.
2. Quantity: The quantity of goods is as stated above under the rubric "Goods submitted for inspection"
3. Price: Seller's final Invoice No. 0107689 dated 3 October 19.. showing a CFR value of US$ 20412.00 has been submitted to us and we have compared and found acceptable the FOB value of US$ 19849.97 (say ONE NINE EIGHT FOUR NINE POINT NINE SEVEN U.S. DOLLARS)
4. Loading: Scheduled to be shipped at Plymouth on board S.S. Morning Star as per B/L No. D5 dated September 25th 19..

REMARKS

This document is valid only if signed by an authorised representative of Trueworth Ltd and accompanied by the following documents:
- negotiable bill of lading or equivalent evidence of shipment to the USA
- copy of Seller's Final Invoice certified by Trueworth Ltd

This Clean Report of Findings in no way releases the Sellers from their contractual obligations to the Importers.

Yours faithfully
TRUEWORTH LTD - ASSESSORS
...

comply with übereinstimmen mit
inasmuch as insoweit als
mandate *hier:* Auftrag
rubric Rubrik
final invoice endgültige Rechnung
find acceptable annehmbar, in Ordnung finden
scheduled geplant
ship verschiffen
B/L = bill of lading Konnossement
authorised ermächtigt, bevollmächtigt
negotiable bill of lading begebbares (negoziierbares) Konnossement
equivalent gleichwertig
certify beglaubigen
release from befreien von
contractual obligation vertragliche Verpflichtung
obligation to Verpflichtung gegenüber

38 Auftragsbestätigung des Spediteurs
Freight forwarder confirms order

➡ Brief 37

Intertrans Ltd
Units 2–10
Marine Walk
Plymouth
PL1 4RF

Our ref: 0123/34218Z
12 January 19..

Cornwall Plastics Ltd
49 Torrington Road
Penzance
Cornwall PE3 9IK

Dear Sirs

We are pleased to confirm that your shipping and on-carriage instructions regarding the consignment mentioned below will be complied with as requested.

The documentation relating to the consignment will be forwarded to you in accordance with your wishes as stated in our previous correspondence.

Consignor: Cornwall Plastics Ltd
49 Torrington Road
Penzance
PE3 9IK
Cornwall

Consignee: Slumberland Foam Inc.
92 Fence Rail Road
Pittsburgh
Pennsylvania PA49721
USA

Consignment: 2,400 kg (20 drums) polyester of silicic acid

.../2

shipping instructions Verschiffungsanweisungen
on-carriage instructions Weiterbeförderungsanweisungen
consignment Sendung
comply with entsprechen, befolgen
relating to sich beziehend auf
forward senden, schicken
in accordance with in Übereinstimmung mit
consignor Übersender, Konsignant
consignee Empfänger, Konsignatar
silicic acid Kieselsäure

2/

Marks: CP/PSA92/1-20

Total weight: 4,543.00 kg

Shipped on: 10 January 19..

Vessel: M.S. Morning Star

Destination: Pittsburgh, Pennsylvania, USA

Should any delay arise or any change in procedure prove necessary, we will notify you as appropriate.

Assuring you of our best attention at all times

Yours faithfully
INTERTRANS LTD

Philip Jones
Manager

cc: Thomas Branscope
Industrial Shipments Dept.

mark Markierung
vessel Schiff
M.S. = motorship Motorschiff
destination Bestimmungsort
delay Verzögerung
arise auftreten
procedure Vorgehen, Verfahrensweise
prove necessary sich als notwendig erweisen
notify benachrichtigen
as appropriate in geeigneter Weise

39 Auftragsbestätigung
Confirmation of order

10 August 19..

B. & A.Trade und Export GmbH
Niederkasseler Lohweg 12
40547 Düsseldorf
Germany

Gentlemen:

Your Order of July 30

Thank you for the above-mentioned order for 500 3.5" Superlite Disk-Boxes as described in the August edition of Chip-Talk USA.

We have mailed the merchandise to you by surface mail and debited $960 to your account as stated. We expect the goods to arrive by the end of the month.

We look forward to the pleasure of doing further business with you in the near future.

Sincerely yours,

Marvin J. Wallis
Export Sales

as described
wie beschrieben
edition
Ausgabe
mail
(per Post) schicken
surface mail
(gewöhnliche) Postzustellung
debit
belasten

Spediteur fordert Versanddokumente für Zollabfertigung an
Freight forwarder requests documents for custom clearance

40

➡ Briefe 41–47

EUROFREIGHT LTD
49 Tenterlowe Lane
Hillingdon
Middlesex MU8 8DE

AG/MM
24 March 19..

Glaxo Chemicals Ltd
237 Sutton Common Road
London SW11 3BY

Dear Sirs

Export Consignment to Budapest, Hungary

We refer to the following shipping order:

Consignee:	Budapesti Vegyi Müvek Budapest XII Radnoti Miklos Utca 23 1367 Magyarorszag (Hungary)
Consignment:	10,565 kg bitumen (15 drums) (value £13,300)
Order No.:	191/1.93 (as per your fax of 12 March ..)
Delivery:	3–4 weeks after receipt of L/C
Hauliers:	Ungarocamion, Budapest

Your customer, Budapesti Vegyi Müvek, has requested us to collect the above consignment using Ungarocamion hauliers and forward it in accordance with his instructions to Hungary.

Please therefore let us have details of either the

.../2

shipping order *hier:* Verschiffungs-, Versandauftrag
haulier LKW-Spediteur
L/C = letter of credit Akkreditiv
documentary collection Dokumenteninkasso
B/E = bill of exchange Wechsel
Bs/L = bills of lading Konnossemente

2/

L/C or the documentary collection (B/E, Bs/L) agreed, to enable us to progress forwarding arrangements and issue a forwarder's receipt.

For customs clearance we require:

For Export

- Export notificaton or export declaration

For Import into Hungary

- Commercial Invoice in triplicate
- Packing specification in triplicate

Should you require any further details or information please do not hesitate to call us on 0181 580 4971 or fax us on 0181 580 4862.

Yours faithfully
EUROFREIGHT LTD

Arnold Graham
Transport Controller

progress vorantreiben
forwarding arrangement Versandvereinbarung
issue ausstellen
forwarder's receipt Spediteurübernahmebescheinigung
customs clearance Verzollung
export notification Exportbenachrichtigung
hesitate zögern

Empfangsanzeige eines Inkassoauftrags
Confirmation of receipt of collection order

41

➡ Briefe 40, 42–47

Benson Bank Plc
6 Feather Lane
London
EC2 7HK

Our ref.: ATX 4977124
20 February 19..

Glaxo Chemicals Ltd
237 Sutton Common Road
London
SW11 3BY

Dear Sirs

We confirm receipt of the documents listed below for collection. Collection will be in accordance with your instructions and subject to our General Terms of Trade.

Your ref.:	ZBD Mr Johnson 0078911
Our ref.:	ATX 4977124
Drawee:	Budapesti Vegyi Müvek Budapest XII Radnoti Miklos Utca 23 1367 Magyarorszag (Hungary)
Collecting Bank:	Hungarian National Bank Foreign Trade Section Szabadsag Ter 8 1850 Budapest Hungary
Payment:	at sight
Amount:	£13,300 + our charges

.../2

collection Inkasso
in accordance with in Übereinstimmung mit
subject to gemäß
drawee (Wechsel-) Bezogener
collecting bank Inkassobank
Foreign Trade Section Auslandsabteilung
payment at sight Zahlung auf Sicht
amount Betrag
charges Gebühren

2/

Documents: Commercial Invoice 5/5
Forwarder's receipt 1/1
Certificate of origin 1/1
Cert. of analysis 1/1
Bill of exchange 1/1

This confirmation of receipt is also a copy of our collection order. Please notify us immediately in the event of discrepancies.

Yours faithfully
BENSON BANK PLC

Terence Hill
Foreign Trade Section

Encs

commercial invoice Handelsfaktura
forwarder's receipt Spediteurübernahmebescheinigung
certificate of origin Ursprungszeugnis
certificate of analysis Analyse-Zertifikat
bill of exchange Wechsel
discrepancy Unstimmigkeit

Inkassoauftrag
Collection order

➡ Briefe 40, 41, 43–47

1 March 19..

Hungarian Business Bank
Foreign Trade Section
Szabadsag Ter 8
1850 Budapest
Hungary

Dear Sirs

We enclose the documents listed below for collection:

Commercial invoice	5/5
Forwarder's receipt	1/1
Certificate of origin	1/1
Certificate of analysis	1/1
Bill of exchange	1/1

The above-mentioned is in respect of a consignment of 15 drums of bitumen (value £13,300) to be shipped on March 8, 19.. from London to Budapest. Delivery of the goods is to be taken by the drawee.

Please release the documents on payment of the draft and arrange to have the proceeds of the transaction by S.W.I.F.T. or by airmail to our Lombard Street branch quoting reference No. ATX 4977124.

Please confirm receipt by S.W.I.F.T. or on the enclosed form. In the event of non-payment please advise us by S.W.I.F.T. or, should this not be possible, by airmail.

This order is subject to the "Uniform Rules for Collections" (1978 revision) International Chamber of Commerce Publication No. 322.

Yours faithfully
BENSON BANK plc
...

commercial invoice Handelsfaktura
forwarder's receipt Spediteurübernahmebescheinigung
certificate of origin Ursprungszeugnis
certificate of analysis Analyse-Zertifikat
bill of exchange Wechsel
drawee Bezogener
draft *hier:* Wechsel
proceeds Erlös
S.W.I.F.T. Society for Worldwide Interbank Financial Telecommunication Bankencomputersystem für internationale Überweisungen
Uniform Rules for Collections Einheitliche Richtlinien für Inkassi
International Chamber of Commerce Internationale Handelskammer

43 Reklamation wegen eines Transportschadens
Complaint about damage to goods in transit

➡ Briefe 40–42, 44–47

FACSIMILE COVER SHEET	
BUDAPESTI VEGYI MÜVEK	
From: Georg Zold Goods Inwards	To: Mr Terence Stamp Export Sales Manager Glaxo Chemicals Ltd London SW11 3BY ENGLAND
Fax No.: 01 6689	Fax No.: 0181 990 6752
Our ref.: UNG/009.92	Your ref.:
Date: 20 April 19..	No. of pages to follow: 4

Facsimile Cover Sheet Telefax Deckblatt

20 April 19..

Dear Mr Stamp

10,565 kg bitumen (15 drums)

We took delivery of the above-mentioned consignment yesterday (19 April) and regret to inform you that 3 of the drums are badly dented with some leakage having occurred. We enclose photographs of the damage for your information and our insurance agent's survey report.

We suspect that the damage was caused in transit and would be grateful if you would arrange for

above-mentioned obengenannt
be dented eingebeult sein
leakage Auslaufen
occur auftreten, passieren
survey report Gutachten, Bericht
suspect vermuten
in transit beim Transit

replacements to be sent to us – carriage and insurance paid – by the end of the month when the entire consignment is due to be collected and taken to Siberia by our CIS customer.

This is a new customer with whom we hope to develop a substantial volume of business in the future. For this reason we are very concerned that the agreed timetable should not be changed.

We trust this matter can be settled swiftly and expect the replacement drums to arrive in good time to be forwarded.

Yours sincerely
Budapesti Vegyi Müvek

Georg Zold
Goods Inwards

Encs

arrange for sorgen für
replacement Ersatz
carriage Fracht
insurance Versicherung
be due fällig sein
CIS GUS
settle in Ordnung bringen
in good time rechtzeitig
to be forwarded um versandt zu werden

44 Verweisung einer Beschwerde an den Spediteur
Referral of customer complaint to freight forwarder

→ Briefe 40–43, 45–47

Your ref.: UNG/009.92
Our ref.: TS/tt

21 April 19..

Budapesti Vegyi Müvek
Budapest XII
Radnoti Miklos Utca 23
1367
Hungary

Dear Mr Zold

15 Drums of Bitumen (10,565 kg)

Thank you for your fax dated 20 April in which you refer to damage and leakage in the case of 3 of the drums delivered.

We would point out, however, that according to the forwarder's receipt all 15 drums were accepted for delivery in good order and can therefore only conclude that the damage occurred in transit whilst the goods were in the custody of Eurofreight Ltd, the haulage company. We therefore suggest you contact Eurofreight Ltd, who, in the light of our previous dealings with this company, will undoubtedly settle the matter swiftly and amicably.

As soon as liability has been established we will supply appropriate replacements. Alternatively, we are willing to despatch replacements immediately, carriage forward. Should you wish us to do so please fax us to this effect.

Yours sincerely
GLAXO CHEMICALS LTD

Terence Stamp
Export Sales Manager

damage Schaden
leakage Auslaufen
forwarder's receipt Spediteurübernahmebescheinigung
in good order ordnungsgemäß, in gutem Zustand
be in the custody of im Gewahrsam sein von
haulage company (Lkw)Transportfirma
in the light of angesichts
swiftly schnell
amicably freundschaftlich
liability Haftpflicht, Haftung
establish feststellen
carriage forward unfrei
to this effect in diesem Sinn, diesbezüglich

Beschwerde über Transportschaden
Complaint about damage in transit

45

➡ Briefe 40–44, 46, 47

Our ref.: UNG/009.92.1
28 April 19..

Eurofreight Ltd
49 Tenterlowe Lane
Hillingdon
Middlesex
MU8 8 DE
ENGLAND

Dear Sirs

15 Drums of Bitumen (10,565 kg)

We took delivery of the above-mentioned consignment on 19 April and note that 3 drums are damaged with leakage. Our suppliers, Glaxo Ltd., waive liability and claim that the goods were delivered to yourselves in good condition, as evidenced by the carrier's receipt. We therefore have no alternative but to hold you responsible for the damage, which obviously occurred in transit. We include a copy of the insurance agent's report and photographs of the drums for your information.

Glaxo are prepared to supply us with replacements at short notice - carriage forward - in order to enable us to meet our commitments to our customer here. We have instructed them to supply us with 3 more drums and will forward the invoice to yourselves for payment.

We trust this matter will be solved to our mutual satisfaction.

Yours faithfully
BUDAPESTI VEGYI MÜVEK
...

consignment Sendung
waive liability Haftung ablehnen
in good condition in gutem Zustand
evidenced bewiesen, nachgewiesen
carrier's receipt Übernahmebescheinigung des Frachtführers
have no alternative but keine andere Möglichkeit haben als
hold s.o. responsible j-n verantwortlich machen
insurance agent Versicherungsagent
at short notice kurzfristig
to meet one's commitments seinen Verpflichtungen nachkommen
to our mutual satisfaction zu unserer gegenseitigen Zufriedenheit

46 Verweisung einer Beschwerde an den Versicherer
Referral of customer complaint to insurance company

➡ Briefe 40–45, 47

Your ref.: UNG/009.92.1
5 May 19..

Budapesti Vegyi Müvek
Budapest XII
Radnoti Miklos Utca 23
1367
HUNGARY

Dear Mr Zold

Thank your for your letter of 28 April in which you give details of damage to 3 drums of bitumen delivered by ourselves to your company on April 19th. We regret the inconvenience caused and feel you acted correctly by having the damage assessed by your insurance agent.

We have looked into the matter and examined the driver's log for the trip in question and have discovered that our vehicle was involved in a minor accident. The case is currently in the hands of our lawyers and should be settled by the end of the month. Our insurance cover provides for indemnification for any eventuality so we would therefore request you to approach our insurers, whose name and address are as follows:

Accident Insurance Europe
Insurance House
London EC1A 4WW
England.

Please quote policy No. GLX/342-00/93.

We trust the matter will be settled to your satisfaction in due course.

Yours sincerely
EUROFREIGHT LTD
...

inconvenience Unannehmlichkeit
act correctly richtig handeln
have the damage assessed den Schaden feststellen lassen
look into the matter die Sache untersuchen
log *hier:* Fahrtenbuch
vehicle Fahrzeug
be involved verwickelt sein
lawyer Rechtsanwalt
insurance cover Versicherungsdeckung
indemnification Entschädigung
eventuality Möglichkeit
approach *hier:* sich wenden an
policy Police

Schadensmeldung an Versicherung
Making an insurance claim

➔ Briefe 40–46

Budapesti Vegyi Müvek
Budapest XII
Radnoti Miklos Utca 23
1367
Hungary

Policy No.: GLX/342-00/93.
14 May 19..

Insurance Accident Europe
Insurance House
London EC1A 4WW
ENGLAND

Dear Sirs

15 Drums of Bitumen (10,565 kg)

We took delivery of the above-mentioned consignment on 19 April and regret to inform you that 3 of the drums are badly dented with some leakage having occurred. We enclose photographs of the damage for your information and our insurance agent's survey report.

We have so far approached both Glaxo Chemicals Ltd, the suppliers, and Eurofreight Ltd, the haulage company, and as neither of these parties will accept liability we are turning to you on the advice of Eurofreight Ltd to claim compensation.

Please refer to the enclosed insurance agent's survey report for details of the damage and an assessment of the replacement costs. We also enclose copies of all documentation authenticated by the British Consulate in Budapest.

We trust you will send us the necessary claims forms at your earliest convenience to ensure that this matter is settled once and for all.

.../2

insurance agent Versicherungsagent
survey report Schadensbericht, Gutachten
supplier Lieferant
accept liability Haftung übernehmen
on the advice of auf Anraten von
claim compensation Schadenersatz fordern
replacement Ersetzung, Ersatz
documentation Dokumente, Unterlagen
authenticate beglaubigen, beurkunden
claim form (Schadens-)Forderungsformular
ensure sicherstellen
once and for all ein für allemal

2/

We have already incurred losses because of this situation and reserve the right make a claim for them.

We also wish to point out that, should we incur further losses as a result of our customer's cancelling the order owing to delay in delivery, we will also claim compensation for loss of business.

We look forward to your early reply in this matter.

Yours faithfully
BUDAPESTI VEGYI MÜVEK

Georg Zold
Goods Inwards

Encs

incur further losses weitere Schäden erleiden
cancel the order den Auftrag stornieren
delay in delivery Lieferverzug
loss of business entgangenes Geschäft

Bitte um Übersendung einer Proforma-Rechnung

Request for pro-forma invoice

48

15 May 19..

JMJ Engineering
89 Brocks Drive
East Cheam
London SW14 1UZ
ENGLAND

Dear Mr Marshall

Our Order No. 342/93 for Piston Rings

In order to obtain an import licence for the items ordered and to open the L/C, we require a pro-forma invoice containing price estimates and quantities.

We would be obliged if you would send us this by the end of the month to enable us to effect delivery as soon as possible.

Yours sincerely
HAMACHER MASCHINENBAU GMBH

Walter Schlimm
Purchasing Manager

piston ring Kolbenring
import licence Importlizenz
item Posten, Position
L/C = letter of credit Akkreditiv
contain enthalten
estimate Schätzung
effect delivery Lieferung ausführen
Purchasing Manager Einkaufsleiter

49 Bitte um Ausfertigung einer Zollrechnung
Request for a customs invoice to be issued

AM/GH
27 April 19..

New Form Plastics Moulds Ltd
Unit 19
Needham Industrial Estate
Oxford
OX8 7HH
ENGLAND

Dear Sirs

As the value of the plastics moulds ordered by ourselves in our letter of February 28 exceeds £50,000 sterling, we require a customs invoice for the customs authorities here to enable them to assess import duty. We would therefore be most grateful if you would issue this document at your earliest convenience to enable us to complete the necessary formalities at this end.

Yours faithfully
MUTUMBUKO PLASTICS LTD

Arnold Twumasi
Import Manager

plastic mould Plastik-Form(stück)
exceed übersteigen
customs invoice Zollrechnung
customs authority Zollbehörde
to assess feststellen
import duty Einfuhrzoll
at your earliest convenience so schnell wie möglich
formality Formalität
at this end hier, bei uns

Bitte an Lieferanten um Gewährung eines offenen Zahlungsziels
Requesting open account payment terms with a supplier

50

➡ Brief 51

JT/GG
29 March 19..

C. & W. Berry Industrial Paints
Wellford Mill Lane
Leyland
Preston PR5 1LE

Dear Mr Berry

Further to our recent telephone call regarding the supply of industrial paints for our retail outlets throughout the UK, I am pleased to advise you that we are prepared to stock your products for a trial period of 90 days as from the beginning of April.

We feel, for the time being, that open account terms with regular quarterly statements would be most appropriate.

Please invoice us here at Head Office in Manchester for all deliveries to all outlets itemising the goods supplied to show unit and total prices and indicating which of our branches have been supplied.

We trust this arrangement will prove satisfactory and would be pleased to receive written confirmation by mail or fax by return.

Yours sincerely
THE CROWN TRADE CENTRE

John Tidmarsh
Head Buyer

industrial paint Industriefarbe
retail outlet Einzelhandelverkaufsstelle
stock lagern
trial period Versuchszeitraum
open account terms offenes Zahlungsziel
quarterly statement vierteljährlicher Kontoauszug
invoice berechnen, in Rechnung stellen
Head Office Hauptgeschäftsstelle
itemise (einzeln) aufführen, spezifizieren
unit price Einheitspreis
total price Gesamtpreis
Head Buyer Chefeinkäufer

51 Kontenausgleich (Übersendung Kontoauszug)
Settlement of account (sending a statement)

➡ Brief 50

WB/JS
2 July 19..

THE CROWN TRADE CENTRE
23–41 Gresham Road
Manchester MA4 1HQ

Dear Mr Tidmarsh

Please find enclosed our statement of account for the period April 1st – June 30th.

As requested we have itemised all deliveries to include unit and total prices and have indicated which of your stores was supplied in each case.

We have deducted £47.92 from the price of the consignment of "Dawn Beige Coverplus Vinyl" delivered to your Preston branch on June 23rd owing to the poor shade match with the previous batch. We trust this will prove acceptable to you.

Please pay by transfer to our account with the Newtown Bank in Manchester (Account No. 2346731).

We look forward to doing further business with you and remain

Yours sincerely
C. & W. BERRY INDUSTRIAL PAINTS

William Berry
Co-director

Enc

statement of account Kontoauszug
deduct abziehen
consignment Sendung
branch Filiale
owing to wegen
shade Farbton
match *hier:* Übereinstimmung
batch Posten, Partie
acceptable annehmbar
pay by transfer durch Überweisung zahlen

Zahlung durch Banküberweisung (SWIFT)
Payment by bank transfer (SWIFT)

52

IG/PO
26 June 19..

Benson Bank plc
34–38 Market Place
New Malden
Surrey KT3 5TZ

Dear Sir

<u>Our Account No. 789315</u>

Please transfer the sum of

£5,423.00

to the account of Esser & Co., Wirtschaftswerbung GmbH in Witten, Germany in respect of their invoice No. 92/4/AUSL./4093.

The account details are as follows:
Account holder: Esser & Co.
Account No.: 789046001
Branch Code: 45240056

We would be grateful if you would arrange for payment to be effected by SWIFT to ensure that the funds arrive by the end of the month.

Yours faithfully
VANTAGE ADVERTISING

Iain Gowe
European Campaigns Manager

transfer überweisen
account Konto
in respect of bezüglich
detail Einzelheit
account holder Kontoinhaber
branch code Filial-Code, Bankleitzahl
arrange for veranlassen
effect durchführen
ensure sicherstellen
funds (Geld-) Mittel

53 Erste Mahnung
First reminder

➡ Briefe 54–57

AL/GL
12 July 19..

Satic Optik GmbH
Kemnaderstr. 33
58456 Witten
Germany

Attention: Herr Holler

Dear Herr Holler

May we draw your attention to the enclosed brochure containing details of our new multifocal, light-sensitive lenses, which are especially suited for those frequently engaged in outdoor pursuits. We feel that we have "beaten the others past the post" as far as marketing this new, low-price product from the USA is concerned and are sure that it will find a ready market in Germany, the home of high-class optics.

May we also draw your attention to our invoice No. 1892Z/5/93 dated May 1st which, according to our records, is so far unpaid. We feel sure that this is due to an oversight on your part and would appreciate payment within the next few days. If payment has already been effected please disregard this letter.

We look forward to hearing from you soon.

Yours sincerely
NORTHERN OPTICS LTD

Alan Gore
Credit Controller

Enc

brochure Broschüre, Prospekt
contain details Einzelheiten enthalten
multifocal lense Mehrstärkenglas
light-sensitive lichtempfindlich
outdoor draußen, im Freien
pursuit Beschäftigung, Tätigkeit
to beat the others past the post die anderen aus dem Rennen werfen
low-price preisgünstig
find a ready market einen guten Absatz finden
optics Optikartikel

Zweite Mahnung
Second reminder

➡ Briefe 53, 55–57

AL/GL
10 August 19..

Satic Optik GmbH
Kemnaderstr. 33
58456 Witten
Germany

Attention: Herr Holler

Dear Herr Holler

Your Ref.:	023/499
Account No.:	SO/894377
Balance Due:	£4,231.92
Due Date:	15 June 19..

I am disappointed to note that, despite our previous reminder of 12 July, your account with us still remains unpaid. You will recall from our Conditions of Sale that all outstanding balances due to us must be paid within thirty days after receipt of our invoice. By placing an order with us you indicated your agreement to our terms. According to my records no query has been raised with regard to the goods delivered or the accounts rendered.

Under the circumstances I would be grateful if you could arrange for the above sum to be paid by return. Should you fail to do so I shall have no alternative but to add interest to the balance at the rate of 25% per annum as prescribed by our Conditions of Sale.

Yours sincerely
NORTHERN OPTICS LTD

Alan Gore
Credit Controller

balance due Sollsaldo
due date fälliges Datum
conditions of sale Verkaufsbedingungen
outstanding balances ausstehende Salden
within 30 days innerhalb von 30 Tagen
receipt Erhalt
with regard to the accounts rendered bezüglich der vorgelegten Rechnungen
by return umgehend
interest Zinsen
at the rate of 25% per annum zu einem Satz von 25% im Jahr
as prescribed wie vorgeschrieben

55 Letzte Mahnung
Final demand

➡ Briefe 53, 54, 56, 57

AL/GL
18 August 19..

Satic Optik GmbH
Kemnaderstr. 33
58456 Witten
Germany

Attention: Herr Holler

Dear Mr Holler

Balance Due:	£4,231.92
Interest Accrued:	£352.58

Despite repeated reminders your account still remains unpaid. Unless I receive a remittance covering all balances due within four days from the date of this letter I will have no alternative but to instruct our solicitors to take legal action against you.

In this case proceedings will be instigated without further notice to regain the sum owed, the interest accrued for the outstanding period and the costs of legal action.

Yours sincerely
NORTHERN OPTICS LTD

Alan Gore
Credit Controller

interest accrued aufgelaufene Zinsen
remittance Überweisung
instruct anweisen
solicitor Anwalt
take legal action against you gerichtliche Schritte gegen Sie unternehmen
proceedings (gerichtliches) Verfahren
instigate *hier:* einleiten
without further notice ohne weitere Benachrichtigung
regain zurückerstattet bekommen
costs of legal action Kosten des gerichtlichen Verfahrens

Bitte um Prolongation eines Wechsels
Request for prolongation of draft

56

FACSIMILE COVER SHEET	
Satic Optik D-58943 Witten	
From: Herr Holler Sales Manager	To: Alan Gore Credit Controller
Fax No.: 02302 276398	Fax No.: 001772 20936
Our ref.: 023/499	Your ref.: 1892Z/5/93
Date: 2 September 19..	No. of pages to follow: 1

2 Sept 19..

Dear Mr Gore

Account No. SO/894377
Outstanding Balance

Please forgive us for not replying to your letters earlier. We have recently undergone a major restructuring of the company entailing a move to more suitable premises on the outskirts of Witten and a significant rationalisation of staffing levels. This, in turn, has led to a number of problems in the Accounts Department, which has now been entirely re-organised. We are currently dealing with a considerable backlog of administrative matters and have, at the same time, been doing our best

➔ Briefe 53–55, 57

Facsimile Cover Sheet Telefax Deckblatt

undergo durchmachen
restructuring Neuordnung
entail nach sich ziehen
premises Geschäftsräume
outskirts Randgebiet, Peripherie
staffing levels Personalbestand
Accounts Department Rechnungsabteilung
backlog Rückstand, Überhang

to keep up with the unexpectedly large influx of advance orders for our new light-sensitive lenses.

We would, under the circumstances, be grateful if you would permit us to prolong the draft until September 30, by which date we will have remitted all monies owing to you including interest accrued.

We trust you will agree to this proposal. You can rest assured that the matter will be settled by the end of the month.

Yours sincerely

Theodor Holler
Sales Manager

P.S.
Please note the address of our new premises:
Industriestr. 20–28, D-58943 Witten

influx
Zufuhr, Zustrom
light-sensitive
lichtempfindlich
draft Tratte, *im Engl. auch häufig:* (akzeptierter) Wechsel
interest accrued
aufgelaufene Zinsen
proposal
Vorschlag

Gläubiger bereit, Teilzahlung zu akzeptieren
Creditor prepared to accept part-payment

57

➡ Briefe 53–56

AL/GL
3 September 19..

Satic Optik GmbH
Industriestr. 20–28
58943 Witten
Germany

Attention: Herr Holler

Dear Herr Holler

Your Account No.: SO/894377
Total outstanding: £4,584.40

We have received your fax of 2 September.

We find your proposal unacceptable, above all because of the inordinately long period of time that has elapsed since the first of our three reminders (12 July) and your response. This has led us to conclude that you are not interested in maintaining a business relationship with us in the long term.

We are, however, prepared to accept an immediate payment of £2,500 accompanied by a draft drawn on yourselves at 30 d/s for £2,162.75 in respect of the unpaid balance including interest accrued by expiry on October 4th. We enclose our new draft for your acceptance.

Please indicate by return whether you accept these terms or not. Should they prove unacceptable we will immediately initiate proceedings for the recovery of all monies due.

Yours sincerely
NORTHERN OPTICS LTD
...

total outstanding gesamter ausstehender Betrag
inordinately übermäßig
period of time Zeitspanne
elapsed verstrichen
maintain aufrechterhalten
in the long term langfristig
accompanied by begleitet von
drawn on bezogen auf
30 d/s = days/sight 30 Tage/Sicht
expiry Fälligkeit
acceptance *hier:* Akzept
initiate proceedings (gerichtliche) Schritte einleiten
recovery *hier:* Eintreibung

58 Kunde entschuldigt sich für Zahlungsverzögerung
Customer apologises for delay in payment

June 17, 19..

Hudson Mechanical Engineering Inc.
782 Fairweather Street
Boston, Massachusetts 02116
USA

Gentlemen:

We received your letter of 10 June and are sorry that there has been a delay in paying your Invoice No. 094/5/93.

We have unfortunately been hit by the economic downswing in Europe as a whole and in the engineering sector in particular, which has resulted in temporary financial difficulties for our company.

A considerable number of our customers have had to file applications for bankruptcy and, pending decisions in these cases, which could go on for months, we are not in a position to press them for payment. We have, nevertheless, been given assurances by our bankers that part-payment of your invoice is possible.We have therefore transferred 50% of the sum outstanding to your account.

With respect to the outstanding balance we are unfortunately compelled to request you to grant us an extension of a further 30 days for this sum. If you can see your way clear to granting us this facility please send us a draft at 30 d/s drawn upon ourselves to this effect, which we will accept and return to you immediately.

We trust you will understand our predicament, which, as you can see, is entirely due to circumstances beyond our control.

Sincerely yours,

...

economic downswing wirtschaftlicher Rückgang
engineering sector Technikbereich
file an application for bankruptcy einen Konkursantrag stellen
press s.o. for payment j-n auf Zahlung drängen
outstanding balance ausstehender Saldo
draft at 30 d/s (days/sight) 30 Tage-Sichtwechsel
drawn upon ourselves auf uns gezogen
predicament (mißliche) Lage
be due to circumstances beyond our control auf Umstände außerhalb unserer Kontrolle zurückzuführen sein

Bitte um Empfehlung eines Vertreters
Request for the recommendation of an agent

59

28 February 19..

South Western Bank plc
Leadenhall Street
London E.C.1 4 WW
England

Dear Sirs

Request for Assistance with Engaging a UK Agent

We are a major German supplier of fitted kitchen equipment with an annual turnover in the Federal Republic well in excess of DM15m. We have so far been represented in the UK by Messrs Crowther & Tidmarsh, a firm of kitchen suppliers which has now ceased trading owing to the death of Mr Tidmarsh. It is for this reason that we are turning to you to ask for assistance in finding a suitable agent for our products.

The firm or individual in question would sell on our behalf on a commission basis, preferably through an already existing network of retail outlets throughout the UK and possibly Northern Ireland. We feel that a well-capitalised company would be able to stock a sufficient quantity of our products to give an impression of our wide range.

We would therefore be extremely grateful if you could recommend a suitable company. We would, of course, also be pleased if your bank would handle all payments arising from the business an agency network would generate.

We very much hope that you will be able to assist us in this matter and remain

Yours faithfully
KÜCHENSTUDIO MAUERMANN
...

fitted kitchen Einbauküche
annual turnover Jahresumsatz
cease trading aufhören, Handel zu treiben
on our behalf für uns
commission basis Provisionsbasis
network Netz(werk)
retail outlet Einzelhandelsverkaufsstelle
a well-capitalised company eine mit Kapital gut ausgestattete Gesellschaft
to stock auf Lager nehmen
range Produktserie
generate *hier:* mit sich bringen

60 Bewerbung um die Vertretung einer Firma
Application to become an agent for a firm

➡ Briefe 61, 62, 63

Modern Sports Sportkleidung
Bahnhofstr. 112
40489 Düsseldorf
Germany

20 March 19..

Land & Hunter Sportswear Specialists
12 Thames Street
Kingston
Surrey KT1 1PF
England

Dear Sirs

Enquiry about Agency Agreement

In their latest information bulletin our bankers, the Gunzelmann Bank in Düsseldorf, publicised your request to them for assistance in finding an agent for your sportswear in Germany.

We have a comprehensive network of specialised retail sportswear outlets throughout North Rhine-Westphalia and, in addition, have branches in all major German cities. We understand from our bankers that you specialise in durable, waxed cotton clothing, lightweight boots, tents and survival gear. We feel there is excellent potential for such equipment here and, provided the quality is in keeping with our customers' expectations, would welcome an opportunity to market your products in the Federal Republic.

We would appreciate it, if you would send us comprehensive sales literature on your products together with a sample tent, waxed cotton anorak and perhaps any other items you feel will show off your goods effectively.

.../2

agency agreement Vertretervertrag
publicise bekanntmachen
sportswear Sportkleidung
comprehensive groß, umfassend
retail outlet Einzelhandelsverkaufsstelle
branch Filiale
durable haltbar
lightweight boots leichte Stiefel
tent Zelt
survival gear Überlebensausrüstung
potential Möglichkeiten
welcome an opportunity eine Gelegenheit begrüßen

2/

Should you require references, the Gunzelmann Bank in Düsseldorf will be pleased to supply you with any information you may desire.

We feel sure that this could well be the beginning of a successful business venture and look forward to hearing from you in the near future. For your information we enclose a brochure and further details of our organisation.

Yours faithfully
MODERN SPORTS SPORTKLEIDUNG

Theo Kohl
Managing Director

Enc

sales literature Verkaufsmaterial
sample tent Musterzelt
show off effectively wirkungsvoll zur Geltung bringen
successful business venture erfolgreiches Geschäftsunternehmen

61 Angebot einer Exklusivvertretung
Offer of sole agency

➡ Briefe 60, 62, 63

30 March 19..

Modern Sports Sportkleidung
Trautmann & Sander
Bahnhofstr. 112
40489 Düsseldorf
Germany

Dear Mr Kohl

Sole Agency Agreement

Many thanks for your letter of 20 March, in which you express an interest in marketing our goods.

We are, indeed, looking for an agent for our products in Germany and it sounds as if your organisation could well fit the bill. Our products are tremendously successful over here in the UK. Waxed cotton clothing is now all the rage and the market is expanding fast. We enclose the samples you request together with illustrated sales literature and our latest trade price-list. We feel sure that the quality will give you no grounds for complaint, as our products are truly state-of-the-art and used by top mountaineers throughout the world.

The Gunzelmann Bank describes your organisation as sound and efficient and therefore, provided you are satisfied with the samples, all that remains is for our lawyers to draft a sole agency agreement ready for signature.

We suggest a meeting here in Kingston to sign the agreement and to get to know each other a little better.

Yours sincerely
LAND & HUNTER
...

sole agency agreement Vertrag für eine Allein-(Exklusiv-)vertretung
fit the bill ins Konzept passen
tremendously successful ungeheuer erfolgreich
be all the rage die große Mode sein
illustrated sales literature illustriertes Werbematerial
trade price-list Preisliste für den (Fach-)Handel
give no grounds for complaint keinen Grund zur Klage geben
state-of-the-art neuester Stand (der Technik)
sound *hier:* gesund
to draft an agreement einen Vertrag aufsetzen

Bestätigung eines Exklusivvertetungsangebots

Confirmation of sole agency offer

62

➡ Briefe 60, 61, 63

Modern Sports Sportkleidung
Bahnhofstr. 112
40489 Düsseldorf
Germany

15 May 19..

Land & Hunter Sportswear Specialists
12 Thames Street
Kingston
Surrey KT1 1PF
England

Dear Mr Land

Confirmation of Agency

After our very instructive and positive meeting in Kingston we should like to state once again the main points upon which we reached agreement as regards our future co-operation:

1. We are to act as your sole agents in Germany for the agreed period.
2. The conditions stated in the agreement are valid for a period of two years after the date of the agreement.
3. We undertake to trade with no imported products of a similar nature which could compete with the products to which this agreement relates.
4. Account sales will be submitted quarterly and we will accept your drafts on us for the net amount accruing from sales of your products.
5. We undertake to display a representative cross-section of your products in all of our retail outlets

.../2

instructive aufschlußreich
sole agent Allein-(Exklusiv-)vertreter
undertake sich verpflichten
product of a similar nature Produkt ähnlicher Art
compete konkurrieren
account sales *hier:* Verkaufsabrechnung
submit vorlegen
quarterly vierteljährlich
draft Tratte, Wechsel
on us auf uns gezogen
accrue entstehen

2/

in Germany in such a manner as to bring them to the attention of a maximum number of customers.

We trust that you will send us written confirmation of these points in due course and look forward to receiving your draft of the agency agreement.

The final version will need to be translated into German, but that is something which we can organise here in Dusseldorf.

Yours sincerely
MODERN SPORTS SPORTKLEIDUNG

Theo Kohl
Managing Director

cross-section
Querschnitt
retail outlet
Einzelhandelverkaufsstelle
in due course
zu gegebener Zeit
agency agreement
Vertretervertrag

Vertreterbericht
Agent's report

➡ Briefe 60, 61, 62

Modern Sports Sportkleidung
Bahnhofstr. 112
40489 Düsseldorf
Germany

1 November 19..

Land & Hunter Sportswear Specialists
12 Thames Street
Kingston
Surrey KT1 1PF
England

Dear Mr Land

Report on First Quarter Sales

We are pleased to inform you that sales activity has been brisk throughout this first quarter with a balance of DM17,000 in your favour. On presentation of your draft drawn on us for this amount of 30 d/s it will be accepted and returned to you immediately, as agreed.

We feel that our advertising campaign, launched as it was at the end of the summer season, was particularly effective because waxed cotton jackets are most suited to weather conditions at this time of year. The new German TV series bought from Thames Televison entitled "Outdoor Style" featuring prominent British TV personalities wearing your company's anoraks has also certainly had a beneficial effect on sales. We enclose some material from the advertising campaign and press coverage of the TV series for your information.

For the next quarter we expect an even greater turnover, particularly in the bigger men's sizes with

.../2

first quarter sales Umsatz im ersten Quartal
brisk lebhaft
balance in your favour Saldo zu Ihren Gunsten
on presentation bei Vorlage
draft Tratte, Wechsel
advertising campaign Werbekampagne
waxed cotton gewachste Baumwolle
feature zeigen
beneficial nützlich, vorteilhaft
sales Umsatz, Verkäufe
turnover Umsatz

2/

large waist measurements. Please make sure that these sizes are available in greater numbers to accommodate the market here.

As regards pricing policy, we feel that the current weakness of the pound should be passed on to our customers and suggest an across-the-board price reduction of 10% on the trade prices quoted.

We look forward to your comments on this matter and are confident that the market will continue to offer considerable potential for the foreseeable future.

Yours sincerely
MODERN SPORTS SPORTKLEIDUNG

Theo Kohl
Managing Director

Encs

waist measurement Taillemaß
accommodate entgegenkommen
pricing policy Preispolitik
across-the-board global
trade price Preis an den (Fachhandel)
potential Möglichkeit(en)
foreseeable future absehbare Zukunft

Erkundigung über Versicherungssätze
Enquiry about insurance rates

64

➡ Briefe 65, 66

5 April 19..

Sovereign Assurance Ltd
London Regional Marine Branch
24 Lime Street
London EC3 7JE

Dear Sir or Madam

Please let us have your quotation for insurance cover against all risks, warehouse to warehouse, for a consignment of:

50 bales of raw silk from Liverpool to Marseille on board the vessel "M.S. Northern Star" of the M&P Line.

Replacement value is £5,000.

Cover is required as from June 1st.

Yours faithfully
Turnpike Trading Co. Ltd.

Ronald Soames
Director

quotation (Preis-)Angebot
insurance cover Versicherungsdeckung
warehouse Lager
consignment Sendung
bale Ballen
raw silk Rohseide
replacement value Ersatzwert
as from ab *(zeitlich)*

65 Versicherungsangebot
Insurance quotation

➡ Briefe 64, 66

10 April 19..

Turnpike Trading Co. Ltd.
Unit 5
Watery Lane Trading State
Gunnerbury
Middlesex MI5 3TH

Dear Sirs

Thank you for your letter of 5 April, in which you ask for our quotation for:

Risk:	50 bales of raw silk, Liverpool – Marseille
Vessel:	M.S. Northern Star
Shipping company:	M&P Line
Value:	£5,000
Cover:	all risks, warehouse to warehouse
Dates:	as from 1 June 19..

We are please to quote you as follows:

15p%

This offer is subject to the silk being seaworthily packed.

We look forward to your reply to this quotation and remain

Yours faithfully
SOVEREIGN ASSURANCE LTD
...

risk Risiko
bale Ballen
raw silk Rohseide
vessel Schiff
shipping company Reederei
value Wert
cover Deckung
be subject to unterliegen
be seaworthily packed seemäßig verpackt sein
quotation Angebot

Abschluß einer Versicherung
Taking out insurance cover

➡ Briefe 64, 65

20 April 19..

Sovereign Assurance Ltd
London Regional Marine Branch
24 Line Street
London EC3 7JE

Dear Sirs

Thank you for your quotation of 10 April for warehouse to warehouse cover for a consignment of 50 bales of raw silk from Liverpool to Marseille to be shipped on or after June 1st.

We are pleased to accept your quotation and would request you to forward the necessary documents to us for the policy to be signed.

We have taken note of your stipulation that seaworthy packing is necessary and will ensure that this is provided.

Yours faithfully
TURNPIKE TRADING COMPANY LTD

Ronald Soames
Director

consignment
Sendung
on or after
am oder nach dem
quotation
(Preis-)Angebot
policy Police
take note of
zur Kenntnis nehmen
stipulation
hier: Bedingung
seaworthy packing
seemäßige Verpackung
ensure
sicherstellen
provide
besorgen, zur Verfügung stellen

67 Erneuerung der Abschreibe-Police
Renewal of floating policy

15 May 19..

Pacific European Timber Export Ltd
White Cross
Cameron House
Lancaster
LA4 T76

Dear Sirs

Renewal of Floating Policy No. 896/3/93

Thank you for your letter of May 10th in which you request the above-mentioned floating policy covering shipments of timber from Singapore to UK ports be renewed.

We hereby confirm that warehouse to warehouse cover has once again been provided for by ourselves to the value of £40,000.

Yours faithfully
CONDOR INSURANCE (U.K.) LTD

Ralf Barrow
Commercial Policies Division

shipment
hier: Ladung
timber
Holz
renew
erneuern
to the value of
im Wert von
Commercial Policies Division
Abteilung für Handelspolicen

Änderung der Rechtsform einer Gesellschaft
Changing the legal form of a company

68

12 March 19..

Messrs Porter & Jones
Solicitors
41 Leadbetter Lane
London EC3 9PP

Dear Sirs

We have pleasure in informing you, as valued customers of long standing, that "Infotec", which has hitherto traded as a sole proprietorship will, as from June 1st of this year, commence trading as a private limited company under the name, "Infotec Ltd".

You may rest assured that the high standard of personal attention and consultancy afforded to our customers in the past will be maintained and, indeed, underpinned by a broader spread of expertise and experience.

Enclosed you will find our "Customer Services" brochure itemising our enhanced range of services and providing biographical details of the new co-directors we have been fortunate enough to have join us.

Please do not hesitate to contact us should you have any queries as regards your firm's requirements or any other matter of concern.

All service contracts extending beyond May 31st will be amended to include the company under its new name and forwarded to our customers for signature.

We look forward to the pleasure of serving you soon.

Yours faithfully
INFOTEC
...

valued customer geschätzter Kunde
of long standing mit langjährigem guten Ruf
hitherto bisher, bis jetzt
sole proprietorship Einzelunternehmen
private limited company (Ltd) (britische) Gesellschaft mit beschränkter Haftung
rest assured versichert sein
underpin unterstützen
a broader spread ein größerer Umfang
expertise Fachwissen, Expertise
range of services Palette der Dienstleistungen
biographical details biographische Einzelheiten
service contract Dienstleistungsvertrag

69 Eröffnung einer neuen Filiale
Opening a new branch

Britannia Rock Building Society
24–26 Old Cattle Market
Manchester
MA6 7BR

15 April 19..

Mr & Mrs William Galsworthy
42 Acacia Avenue
Rotherham
RO1 4IK
Lancashire

Dear Mr and Mrs Galsworthy

Opening of a New Branch

We have great pleasure in announcing that we shall shortly be opening a new branch of the *Britannia Rock Building Society* within easy reach of your home address.

We are now handling such a large volume of accounts in the north of England that it has proved necessary to expand our activities to cope with the ever-increasing demand for our services.

The new Branch Manager in Rotherham, Mr Terence Birchall, has had many years experience in the field of property acquisition and finance and would welcome an opportunity to meet you personally.
He would therefore like to invite you to the new branch's open day on Monday, May 1st between 10 am and 3.30 pm when the *Britannia Rock* will be pleased to extend its hospitality to all visitors caring to participate in light refreshment.

Our Head Office in Manchester, which currently

.../2

branch Filiale
within easy reach leicht erreichbar
handle verwalten
volume Umfang
account Konto
prove necessary sich als notwendig herausstellen
ever-increasing demand ständig steigende Nachfrage
Branch Manager Filialleiter
property acquisition Erwerb von Liegenschaften
hospitality Gastfreundschaft
participate teilnehmen
light refreshment leichte Erfrischung
transfer übertragen

2/

holds your account, will be sending you our "New Option" form, which will enable you to transfer your account to the Rotherham Branch with a minimum of formalities, should you so wish. Customers opting to retain their account in Manchester are, of course, at liberty to do so. The choice is entirely up to you. For your information we enclose details of some of the new services which will be available at all our branches from the autumn of this year.

We look forward to meeting you in May and would also like to take this opportunity to thank you for the trust you have placed in us in the past.

Yours sincerely
BRITANNIA ROCK BUILDING SOCIETY

Hardy Winter
Chief Executive

Enc

formality Formalität
opt wählen
retain behalten
be at liberty to do s.th. frei wählen können, etw. zu tun

70 Änderung der Firmenanschrift
Change of firm's address

21 July 19..

Harvard Plastics Ltd
100–110 Heavytree Lane
Penzance PE2 6ZZ
Cornwall

Dear Sir or Madam

Please note that our firm will be trading from a new address as from August 15 and address all future correspondence to:-

Trelawney Plastic Moulds Ltd
Units 1–4
Rusholm Bridge Trading Estate
Penzance PE2 8PU

Our telephone and fax numbers remain unchanged.

Yours faithfully

P. J. O'Sullivan (Ms)
Communications Manager

note
hier: zur Kenntnis nehmen
trade
Handel treiben
plastic mould
Plastikform
trading estate
Gewerbegebiet
remain unchanged
unverändert bleiben

Geschäftsaufgabe
Closing down a business

71

1 February 19..

Southall Groceries
42 Clarence Parade
Southall
Middlesex MX3 6ZZ

Dear Sirs

It is our sad duty to inform you that for personal reasons The Hackney Trading Company Ltd will be dissolved as from June 1st. This is due to the fact that the principal shareholder and director, Mr Terence Newbury, will be retiring at the end of May and the other members are, for personal reasons, not in a position to take over the running of the company.

The company will be dissolved in the customary manner as prescribed by the Companies Acts (1948–81) with Mr Terence Newbury acting as liquidator for a period of one year.

All outstanding orders will be executed in accordance with existing contracts.

New orders can be placed until March 31 of this year.

We wish to take this opportunity to thank you for the loyalty you have shown towards our company and assure you that we will also be pleased to answer any queries you may have regarding your contracts or any other matters arising.

Yours faithfully
THE HACKNEY TRADING COMPANY LTD
...

dissolve auflösen
principal shareholder Hauptgesellschafter
retire in den Ruhestand gehen
running *hier:* Leitung
customary üblich
prescribe vorschreiben
Companies Act (britisches) Gesetz zur Regelung des Gesellschaftsrechts
liquidator Liquidator, Masseverwalter
outstanding order ausstehender Auftrag
existing order bestehender Auftrag
loyalty Treue, Loyalität
arise sich ergeben, auftauchen

72 Bewerbung um eine Stelle
Job application

➡ Brief 73

15th June 19..

The Manager
Air Space Freight Forwarding
100 Thornbury Road
Newcastle
England

Dear Sir or Madam

I am writing in reply to your advertisement in the European News of June 12th for the post of Sales Manager in your European Division.

I am aged 27, of German nationality, single, bilingual German/English and am currently employed as Freight Co-ordinator with Federal Express (Deutschland) in Düsseldorf where I am responsible for freight movements to and from the US and the UK. I have held this post for three years now and would welcome an opportunity to work in Britain.

I now have a total of 5 years' work experience in freight forwarding, having completed a 2 1/2-year training course as a freight forwarder with Kühne & Nagel, Dortmund, where I stayed for a further two years after completing my training period before taking up my current post at Federal Express.
My current performance-related salary is in excess of £30K p.a.

I enclose a full curriculum vitae and the names of two referees as stipulated.

I look forward to your reply at your earliest convenience.

Yours faithfully
...

sales manager Verkaufsleiter
nationality Staatsangehörigkeit
Freight Coordinator Frachtkoordinator
freight movement Frachttransport
welcome an opportunity eine Gelegenheit begrüßen
freight forwarding Frachtversand
freight forwarder Spediteur
performance-related leistungsbezogen
£ 30K p. a. £ 30.000 pro Jahr *(K = 1.000)*
curriculum vitae Lebenslauf
referee *hier:* Auskunftgeber
stipulate festsetzen, verlangen

Einladung zu einem Vorstellungsgespräch
Invitation to an interview

73

➡ Brief 72

21 June 19..

Mr Peter Schulz
Alte Bahnhofstr. 100
44892 Bochum
Germany

Dear Mr Schulz

Thank you for your letter of 15 June in which you submit your application for the post of European Division Sales Manager.

Interviews for the post in question are being held in London at the Novotel at Heathrow Airport during the weekend of July 19–20. We are inviting suitable candidates to attend for a preliminary interview on the Saturday. On the Sunday short-listed candidates will then proceed to a second round of interviews conducted by a panel made up of our Human Resources Manager and staff.

All short-listed candidates will be notified approximately 10 days after interview.

Travel and accommodation expenses will be borne by the company for all candidates living outside the UK who are invited to interview.

Please confirm your participation by return, indicating your time of arrival.

Yours sincerely
AIR SPACE FREIGHT FORWARDING

Henry Fuller
Human Resources Division

European Division Unternehmensbereich Europa
preliminary vorläufig
short-listed in die engere Wahl gekommen
proceed fortfahren, weiterkommen
panel Ausschuß, Kommission
human resources *hier:* Personalabteilung
staff Belegschaft
notify benachrichtigen
participation Teilnahme
time of arrival Ankunftszeit

74 Referenz- und Empfehlungsschreiben
Testimonial

3rd April 19..

<u>**To whom it may concern**</u>

Ms. MARIA SCHNELL

Ms Schnell worked with Technology Transfer Systems Ltd. as Departmental Head in our software development and documentation department during the period from 1 January 19.. to 31 March 19..

After having rapidly taken stock of the resources available in this department, both in terms of manpower and technology, she was able to proceed to evaluating its strengths and weaknesses. Her restructuring of the section led to an immediate improvement in morale and performance resulting in greater efficiency and dedication from all concerned.

The areas for which she took responsibility involved many skills: documenting, typing and layout of a user manual, testing the software system during development and liaising with software engineers as bugs or queries were raised.

Her ability to chair meetings and conduct them in a manner conducive to constructive results has proved invaluable in the course of her three years with our company.

Technology Transfer Systems Ltd will sadly miss the skills and dedication of which Ms Schnell's departure will deprive the company. We do not hesitate to recommend her to any future employer.

Yours faithfully
...

to whom it may concern *etwa:* an alle, die es angeht (bei englischen Zeugnissen oft verwendete Überschrift)
departmental head Abteilungsleiter
software development Software-Entwicklung
take stock Bestandsaufnahme machen
resource *hier:* Mittel
manpower (verfügbare) Arbeitskraft
efficiency Leistungsfähigkeit
dedication *hier:* Engagement
user manual Benutzerhandbuch
liaise Verbindung halten
bug *hier:* Defekt
chair den Vorsitz führen
conducive to dienlich zu, förderlich für

Ablehnung einer Bewerbung
Rejection of an application

September 15, 19..

Mr Jens Grünewald
Rombacher Hütte 93
44795 Bochum
Germany

Dear Mr Grünewald:

Thank you for your letter of September 1, in which you apply for the post of European Sales Coordinator.

Having studied your résumé, references and testimonials we have come to the conclusion that your particular area of expertise lies in transport logistics and human resources management. What we are looking for, however, is a candidate who is an advertising and marketing specialist. For this reason we are unable to offer you the post in question.

As we feel that your skills could be used elsewhere in our European operation, we have passed your application on to our European Transport Dept., where it will be put on file pending a future vacancy.

With best wishes for the future,

Yours truly,
INTERNATIONAL ELECTRONICS INC

Benjamin Rhodes
Personnel Manager

European Sales Coordinator Europäischer Verkaufskoordinator
résumé Lebenslauf
testimonial Zeugnis
transport logistics Transportlogistik
human resources management Personalführung
advertising specialist Werbefachmann
put on file in die Unterlagen kommen, ablegen
pending a future vacancy bis zu einer zukünftigen Vakanz
Personnel Manager Leiter der Personalabteilung

76 Einführung einer Privatperson
Letter of recommendation for a private individual

3 February 19..

National Chiswick Bank Ltd
Chiswick High Road Branch
27 Chiswick High Road
Chiswick
London W4T 6PP
England

For the attention of the Manager

Dear Sir or Madam

As our company has enjoyed excellent relations with your bank in the past we would be most grateful if you could assist our newly appointed Market Research Co-ordinator (U.K. Division), Herr Franz Lahusen, on his arrival in London at the beginning of next month.

He has been entrusted with the task of drawing up energy consumption profiles for major energy users in the process engineering sector in the south of England and would therefore appreciate any assistance your bank can give him as regards potential customers and their suitability. We feel that your wide experience in dealing with corporate customers and the considerable skill with which you have handled our affairs in the past will greatly aid Herr Lahusen in this undertaking.

We wish to take this opportunity to extend our thanks to you in advance for any assistance given to him in this matter and remain,

Yours faithfully
GEA Energietechnik GmbH
...

excellent relation ausgezeichnete Beziehung
newly appointed neu ernannt
market research Marktforscher
draw up entwerfen, erstellen
energy consumption profile Energieverbrauchsprofil
process engineering Fertigungsplanung
potential customer möglicher Kunde
suitability Eignung
corporate customer Firmenkunde
undertaking Vorhaben
extend *hier:* ausdrücken

Einführung eines Vertreters

Letter of introduction for a company representative

77

Europlast AG
Baubergerstr. 28
80997 München
Germany

31 March 19..

New Channel Ltd
Unit 6
Hadrian Industrial Estate
Cambridge CA4 9UJ
England

Dear Mr Rogers

Our New Representive, Mr Arnold Klein

We are pleased to inform you that, as from May 1st of this year, Mr Arnold Klein will be our new representative in the south of England. He will be taking over from Mr Friedrich Schäfer, who will be returning to Germany for a post of responsibility in Eastern Germany.

Mr Klein will be moving to the UK after a highly successful spell in Canada where he represented our interests from January 19.. to March 19... In the course of his employment with our company, Mr Klein has been able to amass an enviable amount of knowledge as regards local market requirements and customers' expectations and his sound technical background has enabled him to diagnose customer needs quickly and accurately.

You may rest assured that the high standard of service you have come to expect from our company will remain available to all our customers and that all contracts, agreements and arrangements be-

.../2

spell *hier:* Aufenthalt
represent interests Interessen vertreten
employment Beschäftigungszeit
amass sammeln
enviable beneidenswert
as regards bezüglich
local market requirements lokale Marktbedürfnisse
customers' expectations Erwartungen der Kunden
sound *hier:* fundiert
technical background technisches Hintergrundwissen
customer needs Kundenbedürfnisse
high standard hohes Niveau

2/

tween yourselves and our organisation will in no way be affected by the new appointment.

Mr Klein will be calling upon you in the near future to introduce himself personally and is looking forward to meeting our existing business partners and also expanding our operation in the UK.

Should you have any queries as regards future arrangements we will be pleased to provide you with any information you may require.

Yours sincerely
EUROPLAST AG

Peter Wirt
European Sales Co-ordinator

arrangement
Vereinbarung
appointment *hier:*
Stellenbesetzung
call upon s.o.
jm. besuchen
introduce oneself
sich vorstellen
operation
hier: Tätigkeitsfeld

NRW Frachtenkontor
Blumenstraße 23–27
44139 Dortmund
Germany

15 April 19..

Balcombes Insurance Loss Assessor,
Surveyors and Valuers
2 Paradise Row
London E2 4PB
England

Dear Sirs

Vehicle Damage and Part-Loss of Load

Please assess the costs arising from the damage to our vehicle Reg. No. DO-KA 385 and its load (motor vehicle components) when it was involved in an accident with an oncoming lorry on the approach road to Dover Eastern Docks on April 12th.

The vehicle and the remaining part of the load were recovered by:

Crowvale Haulage Ltd
(Commerical Vehicle Recovery Services)
Silverdale House
Pump Lane
London W5 7UJ

Tel. 0181 573 2624

at whose premises they can be examined during usual working hours by appointment.

The Dover Constabulary has made a report on the accident and an investigation into the collision

.../2

Surveyor *hier:* (technischer) Gutachter
Valuer Taxator
vehicle damage Fahrzeugschaden
part-loss Teilverlust
load Ladung
motor vehicle component Kraftfahrzeugteil
oncoming entgegenkommend
approach road Zugangsstraße
recover *hier:* bergen
haulage (Lkw-)Transport
commercial vehicle recovery service Bergungsdienst für Nutzfahrzeuge
usual working hours normale Arbeitszeit

2/

is being conducted by Detective Constable Ralf Hayes.

We also enclose on a separate sheet from our insurers, Star Insurance, a list of points which should be considered in your report.

Please submit your report and invoice in triplicate to ourselves as soon as possible to enable us to make a claim to our insurers.

Yours faithfully
NRW Frachtenkontor

Harald Schmidt
Transport Manager

Enc

by appointment nach Vereinbarung
collision Zusammenstoß
detective constable Kriminalwachtmeister
invoice Rechnung
in triplicate 3fach, in 3facher Ausfertigung

Prendergast & Johnson
Investment Consultants
52 Carter Lane
London EC2 6ZG
England

FG/FB
10 February 19..

IBA Investmentfonds GmbH
Hohe Brück 44
60437 Frankfurt am Main
Germany

Dear Mr Kaltwasser

Current UK Stock Market Trends

Yesterday's sharp fall in the value of the pound on the foreign exchange market led to alarm in the City that inflation would increase again and no further interest rate cuts would be forthcoming from the Government.

The decline in the value of the pound against the mark since Britain's departure from the Exchange Rate Mechanism last year is increasing industry's raw materials and fuel bill. This tendency has been strengthened by the pound's loss of value against the dollar. Sterling is currently being traded at DM2.3673 and $1.4155.

General apprehensiveness among dealers has wiped almost £8 billion off share values with the FT-SE-100 index closing 38.7 points lower at 2831.3. There has been a bout of profit-taking, which served to depress share values still further and it is rumoured that a number of debt-ridden

.../2

stock market trend Trend am Aktienmarkt
foreign exchange market Devisenmarkt
interest rate cut Zinssatzkürzung
be forthcoming bevorstehen
departure *hier:* Austritt
Exchange Rate Mechanism Wechselkursmechanismus
raw materials and fuel bill Rohstoff- und Ölrechnung
apprehensiveness *hier:* Sorge
wipe off auslöschen, schlucken
share value Aktienwert

2/

companies are intending to raise finance with rights issues in the near future.

A false rumour about the Kingfisher group's supposed intention to part-finance the take-over of the French electrical retailer Mercier with a rights issue made the group's shares lose 5p, ending the day down at 526p.

The banking sector was slightly depressed by the reversal of hopes on interest rate cuts. All the major banks lost between 9p–17p and there was also a significant volume of profit-taking.

In general, the market is turning defensive and this trend has been borne out by the latest figures from Dawson Europe, whose analysts have detected an underlying downturn in industrial output with only the water sector registering strong dividend growth.

Despite the current downward trend a monthly survey by Gallup of 101 institutions showed that 15% of them intended to increase their holdings of UK equities, up from 7% in January.

We feel it would be advisable to exercise caution for the next week or so until the rights issued have materialised and the Government has given a clear signal as regards its interest rate policy.

Should there be any last-minute developments we will fax you immediately.

Yours sincerely
PRENDERGAST & JOHNSON
...

FT-SE = Financial Times Stock Exchange Index (gibt den Durchschnittskurs von 100 führenden Aktien in GB an)
close ... points lower um ... Punkte niedriger abschließen
bout *hier:* Anfall, Attacke
debt-ridden mit Schulden belastet
rights issue Bezugsrechtsemission
volume of profit-taking Umfang an Gewinnhereinnahmen
bear out bestätigen
industrial output Industrieproduktion
dividend growth Wachstum der Dividende
holdings Anteile
equities Aktienkapital
interest rate policy Zinssatzpolitik

Änderung des Auftrags (Kundenseite)
Customer amends his order

80

August 17, 19..

Hitech Software Inc.
400 Sunnyvale Boulevard
San José
California 94021
USA

Gentlemen:

Our Order of 1 August for 10 Site Licenses for Software Application

We refer to our above-mentioned order for site licenses for your Megamerge application and wish to point out that, at the time of placing our order, Megamerge 3.0 was the latest version commercially available. As you have since brought out Megamerge 3.1 we wish to amend our order accordingly, as we only install state-of-the-art software.

We trust this amendment will not bring about any delay in delivery. Should this be the case please fax us immediately.

Sincerely yours,
ZIMMERMANN INFORMATIK

Jens Zimmermann
Proprietor

site license Anlagen-, Systemlizenz
software application Softwareanwendung
at the time of placing our order zum Zeitpunkt unserer Auftragsvergabe
commercially available im Handel erhältlich
amend ändern
state-of-the-art dem neuesten Stand der Technik entsprechend
bring about mit sich bringen
Proprietor Firmeninhaber

81 Änderung des Auftrages (Kundenseite)
Customer amends his order

HJ/klt
19 July 19..

Europhar International Ltd
115 Gloucester Road
London W4 3HH
England

Attn: Mr William Mason, Export Sales Manager

Dear Mr Mason

Our Order No. 73F/93 Disposable Syringes
of 10 July 19..

With reference to the above-mentioned order we wish to change the quantity required from 10,000 as originally stated to 15,000 disposable syringes.

We trust you will be able to accommodate us in this matter and assume that the conditions agreed still apply.

Please confirm this amendment in writing, stating any change in delivery date. We are willing to accept two part-deliveries (e.g. of 10,000 and 5,000 units) should this prove necessary.

Yours sincerely

Harald Jung
Purchasing Manager

disposable syringe
Wegwerfspritze
as originally stated
wie ursprünglich angegeben
accommodate
entgegenkommen
apply
hier: gültig sein
amendment
Änderung
delivery date
Lieferdatum
part-delivery
Teillieferung
unit Stück, Einheit
Purchasing Manager
Einkaufsleiter

Ablehnung des Auftrages (Lieferantenseite)
Supplier rejects order

12 August 19..

Riverside Organ Studios
50 Station Road
New Malden
Kent KT1 R55
England

Dear Mr Marshall

We confirm receipt of your order for two Vox Z1 47 synthesisers but regret having to inform you that Vox Ltd have now gone out of business – thus making it impossible for us to accept your order.

There is a wide variety of similar instruments on the UK market, however, and for your information we enclose our latest catalogue and price list.

At present orders for the instruments listed can be processed within 4 weeks of receipt of order.

Assuring you of our best attention at all times we remain,

Yours sincerely

Terry Webb
Export Sales

confirm receipt
den Erhalt bestätigen
synthesiser
Synthesizer
go out of business
das Geschäft aufgeben
wide variety
große Vielfalt
instrument
Instrument
process an order
einen Auftrag abwickeln
4 weeks of receipt of order
4 Wochen nach Auftragseingang

83 Beschwerde über die Unstimmigkeit eines Kontoauszugs
Complaint about a discrepancy in a statement of account

11 July 19..

PLANCO LTD
16 Garden Avenue
Harwich
Essex
CO12 4JR
Great Britain

Attn: Ms Anne Howard, Accounts

Dear Ms Howard

Your statement of account no. 5471 of 30 June 19..

Enclosed please find a copy of your statement up to and including 30th June 19.. showing a balance of £230.00 in your favour.

Unfortunately, we think there is a mistake in this statement. You have forgotten to credit us with £50.00, a reduction which you granted us on 5th May 19.. because one case of your delivery covering order no. 3099 arrived here in damaged condition.

Please check this statement again and if you agree with it we shall be pleased to receive your corrected version. We shall then remit the amount of £180.00 immediately to your account by banker's transfer.

Yours sincerely
Sellhuber & Maier GmbH
...

statement of account Kontoauszug
balance Saldo
credit gutschreiben
reduction Nachlaß
grant gewähren
covering *hier:* betreffend, abdeckend
in damaged condition in beschädigtem Zustand
corrected version korrigierte, verbesserte Version
remit überweisen, schicken
by banker's transfer durch Banküberweisung

Beschwerde wegen unreiner Konnossemente
Complaint about unclean bills of lading

84

13 Feb 19..

Thailand Timber Company
Wireless Road
Bangkok
Thailand

Dear Sir or Madam

We have received the B/L and insurance certificate for the consignment of 50 tons of palletised teak on board m.v. "August Moon", which is due to dock in Liverpool at the end of this month.

We note with dismay, however, that the Bs/L include the notation "6 pallets damaged". As you well know, our company sells timber "on water" to European importers and an unclean B/L is only negotiable in exceptional cases. We fail to understand why you did not provide the shipping company with a letter of indemnity as soon as it was apparent that the goods were not in perfect condition.

It only remains to be hoped that the damage is to the pallets and not to the timber. Should the consignment prove unsaleable we will review all future contracts with your company and seek redress for the loss of trade.

Yours faithfully
NORTHERN TIMBER LTD

J. B. Jones
Manager

B/L = bill of lading
Konnossement
insurance certificate
Versicherungszertifikat
consignment
Sendung
palletised teak
palettisiertes Teakholz
m.v. = motor vessel
Motorschiff
notation
Vermerk, Notierung
pallet Palette
unclean B/L
unreines Konossement
shipping company
Reederei
letter of indemnity
Ausfallbürgschaft
unsaleable
unverkäuflich
seek redress
Wiedergutmachung suchen

85 Zahlung per Postüberweisung
Payment by Mail Payment Order

25 February 19..

Sri Lanka Tea Traders
P.O. Box 1974
Colombo
Sri Lanka

Dear Mr Patel

We confirm receipt of the 30 chests of Ceylon Pekoe tea ordered by ourselves on May 15th.

As agreed in the Contract of Sale we instructed the Finchley Branch of the Benson Bank to arrange for payment by Mail Payment Order through your bank in Colombo. Instructions to this effect were mailed to Sri Lanka today and we have been given to understand that you will receive payment in approximately a fortnight's time.

We look forward to doing further business with you in the near future and remain,

Yours sincerely
FINCHLEY TRADING COMPANY

Daljit Singh
General Manager

chest Kiste
contract of sale Verkaufsvertrag
instruct anweisen
branch Filiale
arrange for payment die Zahlung veranlassen
instructions to this effect diesbezügliche Anweisungen
give to understand zu verstehen geben

Trattenavis
Advice of draft

86

March 3rd, 19..

Messrs Miller & Smutts
95-101 East London Roads
Pietermaritzburg
South Africa

For the attention of Mr Ronald Miller

Dear Mr Miller

Advice of Draft re Your Order No. JK8/3/93 for Agricultural Sprinklers

In accordance with the above-mentioned order the 3 irrigation systems ordered have been shipped on board m.v. "Anastasia", CIF Durban. The vessel is due to dock in Durban at the end of this month.

We enclose the following documents:-

Commercial Invoice
Customs Invoice
Copy of B/L

The Durban branch of Benson International will release the original Bs/L and the Insurance Certificate upon acceptance of our draft drawn upon yourselves at 30 d/s.

We trust the sprinklers will arrive punctually and in good condition and look forward to the opportunity of serving you in the future.

Yours sincerely
KÖHLER BEWÄSSERUNGSANLAGEN GmbH
...

agricultural sprinkler landwirtschaftliche Berieselungsanlage
irrigation system Bewässerungssystem
CIF = cost, insurance, freight *(Incoterm)*
commercial invoice Handelsrechnung, Handelsfaktura
customs invoice Zollrechnung, Zollfaktura
copy of B/L = bill of lading Kopie des Konnossements
insurance certificate Versicherungszertifikat
draft Tratte, Wechsel
at 30 d/s = days/sight auf 30 Tage Sicht

87 Zahlungseinstellung infolge unfreiwilligen Konkurses
Cessation of payments owing to involuntary bankruptcy

The Steel Box Company Ltd
Smithington Lane
Smithington
Sheffield SH7 4AG
England

TH/oq
27 February 19..

TGH Bleche Handelsgesellschaft mbH
Rombacher Hütte 99
46821 Bochum
Germany

Dear Sirs

Outstanding Balances Due to your Company to Date

We regret to inform you that the current worldwide recession in the steel industry has led to a collapse in the market for viably priced metal boxes made in Europe. The sad fact of the matter ist that Eastern European and Far Eastern competitors have flooded our traditional sales territory with good-quality products at 75% of our rock-bottom prices.

We, ourselves, are unable to meet our financial obligations with respect to our bankers and suppliers, with the consequence that insolvency proceedings in accordance with the UK Insolvency Act of 1986 have been instituted against us by our first-ranking creditor, Benson Bank Plc.

The liquidator appointed will wind up our company and pay preferential and secured creditors in full. Thereafter, non-prefential trading creditors such as

.../2

outstanding balance ausstehender Saldo
worldwide recession weltweite Rezession
steel industry Stahlbranche
viably priced metal boxes Metallkästen zu durchsetzbaren Preisen
Far Eastern competitor fernöstliche Konkurrenten
sales territory Verkaufsgebiet
rock-bottom price allerniedrigster Preis
insolvency proceedings Vergleichsverfahren
Insolvency Act Insolvenzgesetz
institute einleiten
first-ranking creditor an 1. Stelle stehender Gläubiger

2/

yourselves with unsecured debts will be taken into consideration.

You will be informed in due course of the date of creditors' meeting, which all parties concerned will be invited to attend.

We hope you will appreciate that we are the victims of a situation entirely beyond our control and would stress the fact that we have been given assurances that the liquidator will treat all creditors equitably.

Yours faithfully
THE STEEL BOX COMPANY LTD

Terence Hill
Company Secretary

wind up auflösen, liquidieren
preferential creditor Vorzugsgläubiger
unsecured debts nicht gesicherte (ungedeckte) Schulden
victim Opfer
beyond our control außerhalb unserer Kontrolle
equitably unparteiisch

88 Zahlungseinstellung
Cessation of payments

2 April 19..

Carpendale Wholesale Grocery Supplies Ltd
Unit 6
Highgate Trading Estate
London N8 9IP

Dear Sirs

We regret to inform you that the recent opening and proximity of a new branch of the "Cash & Carry Supergreen" greengrocer's chain has led to a disastrous decline in the trading situation of our business. This, in turn, has resulted in our no longer being able to meet our current and long-term financial obligations.

Our preferential creditors have obtained a receiving order, under the provisions of which we have been granted a month's grace, during which time we have the opportunity to reach an amicable settlement with our non-preferential creditors. Should we not achieve voluntary composition, the court will issue an adjudication order and appoint a trustee to take charge of liquidating our assets.

We would therefore respectfully invite you to attend the creditors' meeting which will take place on April 15 next on our premises.

You may rest assured that each application will be treated on its merits and in good faith.

Yours faithfully
QUICK TURNOVER GREENGROCERIES LTD

Harold Archer
Chief Accountant

wholesale Großhandel
grocery supplies Lebensmittellieferungen
trading estate Gewerbegebiet
trading situation Geschäftslage
preferential creditor Vorzugsgläubiger
receiving order Konkurseröffnungsbeschluß
provision Vorkehrung
an amicable settlement eine freundschaftliche Einigung
voluntary composition ein freiwilliger Vergleich
adjudication richterliche Entscheidung (*über Konkurseröffnung*)
trustee Treuhänder, *hier:* Konkursverwalter

Auftrag auf Aktienkauf
Order for shares

89

➡ Brief 90

14 May 19..

South Western Investment Centre
PO Box 205
Watford DW1 1BP
England

Portfolio No.: D/281248-2-93

Dear Sir or Madam

Please buy positions in the following shares in accordance with the limits indicated. A total value of £15,000 should not be exceeded.

a) TCC Shares	to the value of £5,000
b) EuroRoad Shares	to the value of £1,000
c) PowerGen (rights issue as per allotment letter)	to the value of £9,000
	Total £15,000

Please debit the appropriate amount to my South-Western Investor Account.

Yours faithfully

G. P. Courtney (Dr)

portfolio Portefeuille
share Aktie
total value Gesamtwert
exceed übersteigen
rights issue Bezugsrechts-emission
allotment letter Zuteilungsbrief
debit belasten
appropriate amount entsprechender Betrag
investor account Investorenkonto

90 Halbjährliche Abrechnung über Aktienkauf
Half-yearly share dealing account statement

➡ Brief 89

30 June 19..

Dr G. P. Courtney
Trantenrother Weg 56
58455 Witten
Germany

Portfolio No.: D/281248-2-93

Dear Dr Courtney

PORTFOLIO VALUATION STATEMENT

We are pleased to forward as per the enclosed your Portfolio statement for the first half of 19..

The statement itemises your current investments, their original cost and current market price, their yield and the total value of your holdings. The Contract Notes from share deals concluded in the course of the last week are also enclosed.

All profits accruing have been credited to your SouthWestern Investor Account, which currently shows a net balance of £17,789.95 in your favour.

We look forward to serving you in the future and remain,

Yours sincerely
SOUTHWESTERN INVESTMENT CENTRE

P. K. Hodgkith
Portfolio Manager

Encs

portfolio valuation Portefeuillebewertung
current investment laufende Investition
market price Marktpreis
yield Ertrag
holdings *hier:* Besitz
contract note Effektenkauf- bzw. Verkaufsabrechnung
share deal Aktiengeschäft
accruing profit auflaufender Gewinn
credit gutschreiben
net balance Nettosaldo
Portfolio Manager Portefeuille-Manager

Auftrag zur Ausübung einer Warenarbitrage
Instruction for arbitrage of goods

91

Lowndes Lambert
Trading Group
Bullrush Lane
London E3 8JL

GL/bk
9 June 19..

Hartmann & Ibing
Warenarbitrage
Alsterberg 95
22335 Hamburg
Germany

Dear Sirs

We are currently involved in a dispute with the Schmitt Handelsgesellschaft GmbH, Hamburg, who have refused payment for a consignment of 4,000 sacks of robusta coffee from São Paulo in Brazil. The consignment is currently on board m.v. "Polixenes" in Hamburg.

They maintain, after having taken samples, that the quality of the coffee does not correspond to the description "best quality" as stated in the contract and have appointed an arbitrator to act on their behalf. The company representing their interests is Gebrüder Sohn, Warenarbitrage, in Hamburg. A copy of their report is enclosed.

Our contract with Schmitt provides for arbitrage in Hamburg and for our arbitrator to be notified of the name of Schmitt's arbitrator within 7 days of appointment. In addition, all arbitrators are to be members of the Chamber of Commerce in the city in which the parties involved have registered their companies.

.../2

dispute Streitfall
consignment Sendung
m.v. = motor vessel Motorschiff
take samples Muster (Proben) nehmen
appoint bestimmen, ernennen
arbitrator Schiedsmann
act on their behalf um für sie tätig zu werden
provide for vorsehen
within 7 days of appointment innerhalb von 7 Tagen nach Ernennung
the parties involved die beteiligten Parteien
register eintragen

2/

We would therefore be most grateful if you would act as our arbitrator in this matter. We are of the opinion that the quality of the consignment of coffee in question is well within the limits of the definition "best quality" and would request you to take samples from a large cross-section of the sacks making up the consignment.

We trust you will succeed in upholding our claim in this matter, thus obviating the need for an umpire to be appointed.

Yours faithfully
Lowndes Lambert Trading Group

Gerald Lambert
Director

Enc

be well within the limits durchaus innerhalb der Grenzen liegen
cross-section Querschnitt
make up *hier:* bilden
uphold (unter)stützen
obviate zuvorkommen, verhindern
umpire Obmann, Schiedsmann

Produktspezifikationen in einem Prospekt
Product specifications in a brochure

92

23 August 19..

Dear Customer

Thank you for your enquiry regarding our products. We enclose a current brochure outlining our entire range and will be most pleased to assist you further with your choice of vehicle.

The content of the brochure enclosed is as accurate as possible from information available at the time of going to press. Dimensions, weights and plan drawings are approximate. Leisureworld Caravans (U.K.) Ltd. reserves the right to alter specifications, colours, models and ranges as materials and conditions demand and, consequently, can accept no responsibility for discrepancies between information contained in this brochure and subsequent models. This brochure, therefore, does not constitute an offer by Leisureworld Caravans (U.K.) Ltd.

If, after having studied our sales literature, you require further information, please do not hesitate to contact one of our approved dealers in the U.K., all of whose names, addresses, telephone and fax numbers are enclosed.

We look forward to the pleasure of serving you in the near future.

Yours faithfully
Leisureworld Caravans (U.K.) Ltd.

Harvey Threadgold
General Manager

Encs

outline *hier:* einen Überblick geben
range (Produkt-)Palette
choice Wahl
dimension Abmessung
plan drawing Planzeichnung
reserve the right sich das Recht vorbehalten
alter abändern
consequently infolgedessen
accept responsibility Verantwortung übernehmen
discrepancy Abweichung
subsequent nachfolgend
constitute bilden, darstellen
sales literature Verkaufsmaterial
approved dealer anerkannter Händler

93 Bestellung eines Rechtsanwalts
Calling in a solicitor

Newtown Electronics
36 Barton Road
Hatfield
Herts HT9 7PQ

28 March 19..

Messrs Cotton, Gummersall & Palmer
Windsor House
1008 East End Road
London SW16 7UJ

Dear Sirs

Breach of Contract due to Delay in Delivery

We are writing to you to request you to represent our interests in what we consider to be a clear case of breach of contract.

From the correspondence enclosed you will note that "DV-Electronic Data Systems Deutschland GmbH" have failed to comply with the terms set out in our Contract of Sale (see enclosure), whereby delivery of the goods in question (viz 400 VGA Monitors, Type MultiSync XL) was assured by 15th January 19..

We finally took delivery of these articles on March 10th, by which time we had incurred considerable financial losses and were obliged to supply our customers at 25% under list price.
We have already deducted out losses from the invoice amount + 10% administration charges and transferred the amended invoice amount to DV-Electronic's account. We have, in addition, cancelled a further order (see enclosures) for 400 key-

.../2

breach of contract Vertragsbruch
delay in delivery Lieferverzug
data system Datensystem
set out darlegen
the goods in question die in Frage stehenden Güter
viz nämlich, das heißt
assure zusichern
be obliged gezwungen sein
at 25% under list-price 25% unter dem Listenpreis
deduct out abziehen
invoice amount Rechnungsbetrag
administration charges Verwaltungsgebühren

2/

boards. DV-Electronic, however, are insisting upon a list-price settlement and have indicated that they will not accept our cancellation. They have also passed the matter on to their solicitors, who have threatened litigation, should we fail to honour our order for the keyboards.

We welcome your comments on this matter and would be most grateful if you could act in such a manner as to convince DV-Electronic that any further attempt to press their claim would prove futile.

Yours faithfully
NEWTOWN ELECTRONICS

J. B. Butterson
Managing Director

Encs

pass the matter on to their solicitors die Sache an ihre Rechtsanwälte weiterleiten

threaten litigation mit einem Rechtsstreit drohen

honour an order einen Auftrag erfüllen

94 Bestellung eines Management Consultant
Enlisting the aid of a management consultant

20 July 19..

Messrs Price Waterhouse
Management Consultants
Knightsbridge House
185 Knightsbridge
London SW7 90L

Dear Sirs

As a result of the lasting effects of the current recession, which has affected business badly in our field, we are now obliged to restructure our operation and will have no alternative but to retrench heavily.

We therefore require assistance with the shedding of workers by natural wastage or voluntary redundancy, severance pay, early retirement plans with or without a gratuity, redundancy schemes with retraining opportunities for younger workers and a public relations strategy to help make these inevitable measures more palatable to our employees and the public at large.

In addition, we will need to scrutinize our middle and upper management structures in order to weed out under-productive staff. Here, we will require assistance with assessment procedures to gauge performance and also with the implementation of decisions resulting from the discovery that particular individuals can no longer remain in our employ.

We would therefore request you to contact us immediately with a view to drawing up a profile of our company and putting forward short and medium-term strategies.

Yours faithfully

...

retrench kürzen, sich einschränken
shed workers Arbeitskräfte abbauen
natural wastage natürlicher Abgang
voluntary redundancy freiwillige Freisetzung
severance pay Abfindungszahlung
early retirement plan Frühpensionierungsplan
gratuity Abfindungssumme
palatable schmackhaft
scrutinize gründlich prüfen
weed out aussondern
under-productive staff weniger produktives Personal
assessment procedures Bewertungsverfahren
gauge performance Leistung messen
implementation Einführung

June 25, 19..

Constance Cummings
Cosmetics Manufacturers
One World Trade Center
Suite 7691
New York
N.Y. 10048
U.S.A.

Gentlemen:

We are now in a position to provide you with the first results of our market survey on German consumer habits as regards the use of cosmetics.

Our field-workers conducted a representative survey of females aged 15–60 years and completed a questionnaire with the test persons on their preferences as regards hair and skin preparations. Our survey incorporated questions on the recycling of packaging, vivisection issues and a possible multicultural image of society. In addition, we asked questions on matters such as manufacturing methods and the sourcing of ingredients used for beauty preparations (low-wage labor in the Third World, Amazon rain forest depletion, "natural" and "green" products, herbal remedies, cosmetic substances used by ancient cultures etc.).

Our conclusions and recommendations are set out in detail in the charts included with this letter.

In essence, we recommend that the 15–25 year-old age group be approached with explicit reference to environmentally friendly products, developed on human test subjects and in no way involving the use of animals. Here a synthesis should be achiev-

.../2

market survey Marktstudie
consumer habit Verbrauchergewohnheit
questionnaire Fragebogen
incorporate beinhalten
packaging Verpackung
vivisection issue Thema der Vivisektion
multi-cultural image of society multikulturelles Image der Gesellschaft
manufacturing method Herstellungsmethode
ingredient Bestandteil
the Third World die Dritte Welt
Amazon rain forest depletion Raubbau am Regenwald des Amazonasgebiets

2/

ed between fashion-consciousness and "natural" beauty. We suggest using both European and African models in harmonious but also dynamic and exciting situations in your advertising.

The 25–40 year-olds will probably best respond to an "enlightened" and realistic approach to the problems of "getting the best out of your looks" with a little help from cosmetics. Here, an "intimate" approach is important, i.e. the cosmetic industry is secretly helping you to enhance your looks, whilst unsuspecting males think it's natural (hair rinses, skin toners, anti-wrinkle preparations).

The 45–60 year-olds will probably best respond to even more subtle allusions to the need for nature to be helped along a little, but here we recommend the idea of, "Go on, enjoy yourself now," or, "Treat yourself to something really good!" Prices for this age group can be increased by 5%–10% to underline market segmentation.

We trust you will be able to incorporate our suggestions in your advertising campaign and will be pleased to clarify any of our findings, should you request us to do so.

Sincerely yours,
DAWSON & DAWSON

A. P. Schleifer
Senior Consultant

Encs

herbal remedy pflanzliche Arznei
fashion-consciousness Modebewußtsein
enhance (vorteilhaft) zur Geltung bringen
hair rinse Haarspülung
skin toner Hauttönungsmittel
anti-wrinkle preparation Antifaltenpräparat
allusion Anspielung, Hinweis

➡ Brief 97

HARVARD PLASTICS INC.
Broadway
New York
N.Y. 10018
USA

August 10, 1993

Human Resources Department
Harvard Plastics Inc. (U.K.)
Bull Ring Industrial Estate
Birmingham BI8 9LL
United Kingdom

Gentlemen:

European Languages Drive

As President of Harvard Plastics Inc. I take great pleasure in utilizing this opportunity to address all operatives in the Human Resources Departments of our European subsidiaries. As you all know, the course of history has brought about momentous changes in Europe and we cannot afford to let new chances pass us by. For this reason, we must all re-think, re-structure and react.

To this end I am issuing a Management Directive to all Human Resources Departments to launch an all-out effort to attract multi-lingual personnel at all levels. The logistics at local level are entirely the province of individual Human Resources Managers, but let me make myself clear on this, we need and expect results and an up-to-date profile of all subsidiaries will be drawn up exactly one year from now.

.../2

drive Kampagne, Werbefeldzug
operative *hier:* Angestellter
Human Resources Department Personalabteilung
management directive Managementrichtlinie
an all-out effort eine ganz gewaltige Anstrengung
multi-lingual personnel mehrsprachiges Personal
an up-to-date profile ein auf den neuesten Stand gebrachtes Profil

2/

Existing employees must be encouraged to develop their language skills in their free time in courses run on company premises. Promotion prospects will be made dependent on this. Harvard Plastics are willing to refund employees' outlay on language tuition upon successful completion of a recognised qualification. Extra bonuses will be paid if an employee learns more than one foreign language. Furthermore, additional financial incentives will be made available to promote the study of Eastern European Languages such as Russian, Polish and Hungarian, for I feel that a sales thrust eastwards in the near future can only succeed if our personnel can operate through the medium of the language in the sales territory targeted.

I trust that our European Languages Drive Project will be crowned with success and feel sure that a high degree of response throughout our organization will serve to secure jobs in the future.

Very truly yours,

Clarence C. Pollock
PRESIDENT

language skill Sprachfertigkeit
free time Freizeit
company premises Firmenräume
promotion prospects Beförderungsaussichten
employees' outlay Ausgaben der Angestellten
language tuition Sprachunterricht
recognised qualification anerkannte Qualifikation
sales thrust Verkaufsvorstoß
sales territory Verkaufsgebiet

Bezugnahme auf Jahresbericht der Muttergesellschaft
Response to parent company's annual report

97

➡ Brief 96

Harvard Plastics Inc. (UK)
Bull Ring Industrial Estate
Birmingham Bl8 9LL
United Kingdom

4th July 19..

The President
Harvard Plastics Inc.
Broadway
New York
N.Y. 10018
USA

Dear Mr Pollock

We have studied your Annual Report for 19.. and come to the conclusion that the loss in pre-tax profits of $1.2bn incurred by Harvard Plastics world-wide was mainly attributable to high labour costs and import duty on plastics entering Europe.

The conclusion we have come to is that relocation of part of your manufacturing facilities in one of the cheaper EU countries (UK, Ireland, Portugal, Greece) may be the answer to import duties, for in this way the "80% local content" ruling as regards goods manufactured by companies in non-EU ownership can be complied with. Over 1,000 Japanese companies already have a production site in the UK alone.

We feel that every effort should be made to contact the municipalities in areas designated by the EU as "regional development areas" in order to obtain EU funding and low-priced land. We are convinced that any effort to bring jobs to Europe will be warmly welcomed by the government and local population

.../2

annual report Jahresbericht
loss in pre-tax profits Verlust bei den Vor-Steuer-Gewinnen
bn = billion Milliarde
incur auftreten
relocation Verlegung
manufacturing facilities Herstellungsbetriebe
the 80% local content ruling die Regelung, daß 80% aus heimischer Produktion stammen müssen
municipality städtische Behörde
designate bezeichnen
regional development area regionales Entwicklungsgebiet

2/

concerned, with good chances of highly favourable tax relief arrangements for an initial period and, especially in the UK, a pool of skilled labour available immediately.

Our Public Relations Department has already started to sound out local authorities in suitable areas in the UK and we will be sending you a report of our findings in good time for your AGM on 1 September.

You may rest assured that our recommendations will remain confidential, until such time as the matter of relocation in Europe has been discussed at the highest level.

Yours sincerely

Henry Wilberforce
Chief Executive
Harvard Plastics (UK)

funding Geldmittel
tax relief Steuererleichterung
skilled labour Fachpersonal
sound out aussondieren, herausfinden
AGM = Annual General Meeting Jahreshauptversammlung
confidential vertraulich

Ankündigung der Gründung einer Gesellschaft
Announcing the formation of a company

98

➡ Brief 99

Mediquip
Richmond Industrial Estate
Richmond
Surrey SU9 1JK

12 July 19..

Krankenhaustechnik GmbH
Düsseldorfer Str. 90
45145 Essen
Germany

Dear Sirs

Medical and Surgical Instruments

We are pleased to announce that our newly formed company "Mediquip Ltd", Company Registration No. 2391824, will start trading in Europe as from September 1st.

We specialise in the manufacture and distribution of high-quality medical apparatus and surgical equipment. In addition, we pioneer innovative ideas by inviting selected customers to test new apparatus made available to them at a fraction of cost price, thus making new techniques and treatments available to patients at affordable prices.

Our latest invention is a device for kidney operations without major surgery. Besides this we are currently promoting a local anaesthetic package to cut down the risks associated with surgery normally performed under general anaesthetic.

We include our catalogue and export price list for your information. All prices are quoted FOB UK airport.

…/2

manufacture Herstellung
distribution Vertrieb
selected customers ausgewählte Kunden
make available zur Verfügung stellen
at a fraction of cost price zu einem Bruchteil des Selbstkostenpreises
treatment Behandlung
at affordable prices zu Preisen, die man sich leisten kann
invention Erfindung
device Vorrichtung, Gerät
kidney operations Nierenoperationen
promote fördern
anaesthetic package Narkosepaket

2/

Should you wish to be considered to take part in the testing of new devices please return the enclosed registration form. We would instal such devices at our own cost and offer attractive discounts on other orders to those participating.

We hope that we shall soon be able to supply you with your medical equipment needs. If you have any questions please do not hesitate to get in touch with us.

Yours faithfully
MEDIQUIP LTD

David Vance
Managing Director

Encs

cut down
verringern
perform surgery
chirurgische Eingriffe vornehmen
medical equipment needs
Bedarf an medizinischer Ausrüstung

Gegenangebot
Counter-offer

➡ Brief 98

15 December 19..

Mediquip Ltd
Richmond Industrial Estate
Richmond
Surrey SU9 1JK
ENGLAND

Dear Sirs

Your Offer No. 1093 for Surgical Instruments

Thank you for the above-mentioned offer of December 1st.

We have studied your prices and compared them with those of your competitors and, despite being well pleased with the quality of the goods, must point out that your prices are some 10% too high for the market here.

If you can see your way clear to accommodating us with a 10% reduction we will be pleased to place an order for the equipment listed on the order form enclosed.

We look forward to your response to our proposal.

Yours faithfully
DR. ZANDER KLINIKEN

Michael Schmidt
Manager

surgical instruments chirurgische Instrumente
compare vergleichen
competitor Konkurrent
be well pleased durchaus zufrieden sein
if you can see your way clear wenn Sie eine Möglichkeit sehen
accommodate s.o. j-m entgegenkommen
order form Auftragsformular
proposal Vorschlag

100 Hersteller verweist Kunden an örtlichen Vertreter
Manufacturer refers customer to local agent

17 August 19..

Herrn Michael Bendorf
Am Neggenborn 80
44892 Bochum
Germany

Dear Herr Bendorf

Many thanks for your valued enquiry as regards our range of cabin cruisers.

I have mailed you our brochure today by separate post and I trust it will be of interest. The price list is effective from 1st September 19.. and is for UK specifications.

I have asked our importer, "Auto Theimann & Freizeit", Kohlenstr. 45, 44795 Bochum, Germany to confirm German prices, German specifications and also give you more detail about the products and built quality and other information you require.

In the meantime, if I can be of further assistance please contact me.

Yours sincerely
Mannepower International Ltd

Terence Perkins
Sales & Marketing Manager

c.c. Alfred Prentice

your valued enquiry Ihre geschätzte Anfrage
as regards hinsichtlich, betreffend
cabin cruiser Kabinenkreuzer
be effective gültig sein
specifications *hier:* Normen, Konstruktionsvorschriften
give more detail genauere Einzelheiten geben
built quality *hier:* Fertigungsqualität

Anhänge

Währungen verschiedener englischsprachiger Länder

Land	Währung deutsch	Währung englisch	Abkürzung	Untereinheit
Australien	Austr. Dollar	Australian dollar	A$	100 cents
Bahamas	Bahama-Dollar	Bahamian dollar	B$	100 cents
Barbados	Barbados-Dollar	Barbados dollar	BD$	100 cents
Dominica	Ostkarib. Dollar	East Caribbean dollar	EC$	100 cents
Fidschi	Fidschi-Dollar	Fiji dollar	F$	100 cents
Großbritannien und Nordirland	Pfund Sterling	pound (sterling)	£ (stg)	100 pence
Guyana	Guyana-Dollar	Guyana dollar	G$	100 cents
Hongkong	Hongkong-Dollar	Hong Kong dollar	HK$	100 cents
Indien	Ind. Rupie	Indian rupee	Rs	100 paise
Irland	Ir. Pfund	Irish pound (punt)	IR£	100 pence
Jamaika	Jamaika-Dollar	Jamaican dollar	J$	100 cents
Kanada	Kanad. Dollar	Canadian dollar	C$	100 cents
Liberia	Liberianischer Dollar	Liberian dollar	L$	100 cents
Malawi	Malawi-Kwacha	Malawi kwacha	MK	100 tambala
Malaysia	Malaysischer Ringgit	ringgit	M$	100 sen
Malta	Maltesische Lira	lira, *pl.* liri	LM	100 cents
Mauritius	Mauritius-Rupie	Mauritius rupee	MauR	100 cents
Neuseeland	Neuseeland-Dollar	New Zealand dollar	NZ$	100 cents
Nigeria	Naira	naira	N	100 kobo
Sambia	Kwacha	Zambian kwacha	K	100 ngwee
Seychellen	Seychellen-Rupie	Seychelles rupee	SR	100 cents
Simbabwe	Simbabwe-Dollar	Zimbabwe dollar	Z$	100 cents
Singapur	Singapur-Dollar	Singapore dollar	S$	100 cents
Südafrika, Republik	Rand	rand	R	100 cents
Tansania	Tansania-Shilling	Tanzanian shilling	Tsh	100 cents
Uganda	Uganda-Shilling	Uganda shilling	USh	100 cents
Vereinigte Staaten von Amerika	US-Dollar	United States dollar	(US) $	100 cents

Britische und amerikanische Maße und Gewichte

Längenmaße

1 inch	= 2,54 cm
1 foot	= 12 inches = 30,48 cm
1 yard	= 3 feet = 91,44 cm
1 (statute) mile	= 1760 yards = 1,609 km

Nautische Maße

1 fathom	= 6 feet = 1,829 m
1 nautical mile	= 1,852 km

Flächenmaße

1 square inch	= 6,452 cm^2
1 square foot	= 144 square inches = 929,029 cm^2
1 square yard	= 9 square feet = 8361,26 cm^2
1 acre	= 4840 square yards = 4046,8 m^2
1 square mile	= 640 acres = 259 ha = 2,59 km^2

Britische Hohlmaße

Trocken- und Flüssigkeitsmaße

1 gill	= 0,142 l	
1 pint	= 4 gills	= 0,568 l
1 quart	= 2 pints	= 1,136 l
1 gallon	= 4 quarts	= 4,5459 l
1 quarter	= 64 gallons	= 290,935 l

Trockenmaße

1 peck	= 2 gallons	= 9,092 l
1 bushel	= 4 pecks	= 36,368 l

Flüssigkeitsmaße

1 barrel	= 36 gallons	= 163,656 l

Amerikanische Hohlmaße

Trockenmaße

1 pint	= 0,5506 l	
1 quart	= 2 pints	= 1,1012 l
1 gallon	= 4 quarts	= 4,405 l
1 peck	= 2 gallons	= 8,8096 l
1 bushel	= 4 pecks	= 35,2383 l

Flüssigkeitsmaße

1 gill	= 0,1183 l	
1 pint	= 4 gills	= 0,4732 l
1 quart	= 2 pints	= 0,9464 l
1 gallon	= 4 quarts	= 3,7853 l
1 barrel	= 31.5 gallons = 119,228 l	
1 barrel petroleum	= 42 gallons	= 158.97 l

Handelsgewichte

1 grain	= 0,0648 g	
1 dram	= 27.3438 grains = 1,772 g	
1 ounce	= 16 drams	= 28,35 g
1 pound	= 16 ounces	= 453,59 g
1 hundredweight	= 1 quintal	
Brit.	= 112 pounds = 50,802 kg	
Am.	= 100 pounds = 45,359 kg	
1 long ton *Brit.*	= 20 hundredweight = 1016,05 kg	
1 long ton *Am.*	= 20 hundredweight = 907,185 kg	
1 stone	= 14 pounds	= 6,35 kg
1 quarter		
Brit.	= 28 pounds = 12,701 kg	
Am.	= 25 pounds = 11,339 kg	

Raummaße

1 cubic inch	= 16,387 cm^3
1 cubic foot	= 1728 cubic inches = 0,02832 m^3
1 cubic yard	= 27 cubic feet = 0,7646 m^3

Verzeichnis wichtiger Handelsabkürzungen

a.a.r.	against all risks	gegen alle Risiken
a/c	account	Konto
a/d	after date	nach Dato
AGM	annual general meeting	(Jahres)Hauptversammlung
a.m.	ante meridiem	vormittags
approx.	approximately	ungefähr
art.	article	Artikel
A/S	account sales	Verkaufsabrechnung
ASAP	as soon as possible	möglichst bald
ATM	automated teller machine	Geldautomat
Bdy.	broadway	britische u. amerikanische Straßenbezeichnung
B/E (B(s)/E)	bill(s) of exchange	Wechsel, Tratte
B/L (B(s)/L)	bill(s) of lading	Konnossement, Seefrachtbrief
Bros.	brothers	Gebrüder
c./ca.	circa	ungefähr
CAD	cash against documents	Kasse gegen Dokumente
c.c.	carbon copy	Durchschrift
C.C.	charges collect	Erhebung von Gebühren, unfrei
CFR	cost and freight	Kosten und Fracht
CIF	cost insurance freight	Kosten Versicherung und Fracht
CIP	carriage and insurance paid to	frachtfrei versichert bis
c/o	care of	per Adresse
Co	company	Gesellschaft
COD	cash on delivery	Nachnahme
COS	cash on shipment	Zahlung bei Verschiffung
c.p.d.	charterer pays dues	Abgaben werden vom Charterer bezahlt
CPT	carriage paid to	frachtfrei
cr.	creditor	Gläubiger
c.r.	current rates	zu den Sätzen und Tarifen, die zur Zeit in Kraft sind
Cres.	crescent	britische Straßenbezeichnung
c.t.	conference terms	Konferenzbedingungen
cv	curriculum vitae	Lebenslauf
cwt.	hundredweight	Zentner
D/A	deposit account	Sparkonto
D/A	documents against acceptance	Dokumente gegen Akzept
DAF	delivered at frontier	geliefert Grenze
d/d	days after date	Tage nach dato
DDP	delivered duty paid	geliefert verzollt
DDU	delivered duty unpaid	geliefert unverzollt

dep.	departure	in Flugplänen angegebene Abflugzeit
DEQ	delivered ex quay	geliefert ab Kai
DES	delivered ex ship	geliefert ab Schiff
div.	dividend	Dividende
doz.	dozen	Dutzend
D/P	documents against payment	Dokumente gegen Zahlung
d/s	days after sight	Tage nach Sicht
E.& O.E.	errors and omissions excepted	Irrtümer und Auslassungen vorbehalten
EEA	Exchange Equalisation Account	Devisen-/Währungsausgleichs-konto
EFTPOS	Electronic funds transfer at the point of sale	Einzugsermächtigung am Kassenterminal
e.g.	exempli gratia, for example	zum Beispiel
EMS	European Monetary System	Europäisches Währungssystem
EMU	European Monetary Union	Europäische Währungsunion
encl, enc(s)	enclosure(s)	Anlage(n)
E.O.M.	end of month	Monatsende
ERM	Exchange Rate Mechanism	Wechselkursmechanismus
ETA	estimated time of arrival	planmäßige Ankunftszeit
etc.	et cetera, and so on	usw.
e.t.c.	expected to complete	zu erwartendes Löschende
e.t.s.	expect to sail	voraussichtliche Abfahrt
EXW	ex works	ab Werk
f.a.q.	fair average quality	Durchschnittsqualität
FAS	free alongside ship	frei Längsseite Seeschiff
FCA	free carrier	frei Frachtführer
FCR	forwarding agent's certificate of receipt	Spediteur- Übernahme-bescheinigung
FCT	forwarding agent's certificate of transport	Spediteur- Übernahme-bescheinigung
FIFO	first in first out	Zuerstentnahme der älteren Bestände
FOB	free on board	frei an Bord
FPA	free from particular average	frei von Teilschäden außer im Strandungsfall
ft. (')	foot, feet	Fuß
FTSE	Financial Times Stock Exchange Index	britischer Aktienindex
Gds.	gardens	britische Straßenbezeichnung
HGV	heavy goods vehicle	Lastkraftwagen (LKW)
HMS	Her (His) Majesty's Ship (Steamer)	Ihrer (Seiner Majestät) Schiff (Dampfer)
H.P.	horse power	PS, Pferdestärke
HP	hire purchase	Mietkauf

ICC	institute cargo clauses	Versicherungsbedingungen für Gütertransporte
i.e.	id est, that is to say	das heißt
IMO	International Money Order	Internationale Zahlungsanweisung
in. (")	inch	Zoll
Inc.	incorporated with limited liability (AE)	GmbH, AG
incl.	including	einschließlich
INCOTERMS	international commercial terms	internationale Regeln für die Auslegung handelsüblicher Vertragsformeln
IOU	"I owe you"	Schuldschein
kg	kilogram	Kilogramm
lbs (lbs)	pound(s)	Pfund
L/C (L(S)/C)	letter(s) of credit	Akkreditiv
LIFO	last in first out	Zuerstentnahme der neuesten Bestände
Ltd.	limited	mit beschränkter Haftung
m/d	months after date	Monate nach Dato
MLR	minimum lending rate	Mindestdiskontsatz
M.O.	money order	Postanweisung
Mr	mister	Herr
M/R	mate's receipt	Empfangsquittung, Bescheinigung, daß sich die Ware an Bord befindet
Mrs		Anrede einer verheirateten Frau
m/s	months after sight	Monate nach Sicht
Ms		Anrede einer Frau, ohne anzugeben, ob sie verheiratet ist oder nicht.
MS	motor ship	Motorschiff
MV	motor vessel	Motorschiff
N/A	not applicable	nicht zutreffend
nd (2nd)	second	zweiter/-e/-es
No/Nos	number(s)	Nr.
O/o	to the order of	an die Order von
oz (oz(s))	ounce(s)	Unze(n)
p.a.	per annum	jährlich
pc (pc(s))	piece(s)	Stück
pd	paid	bezahlt
PIN	personal identity number	persönliche Geheimzahl
plc	public limited company	Aktien-, Kapitalgesellschaft
p.m.	post meridiem	nachmittags
P.O. Box	Post Office Box	Postfach

P.O.	postal order	Postanweisung
p.o.d.	paid on delivery	bezahlt bei Anlieferung
pp	per pro (curationem)	im Auftrag; in Vertretung; per Prokura
ppd	pre-paid	im voraus bezahlt
p.t.o.	please turn over	bitte wenden
Pty	proprietary company, a private limited company registered in South Africa or Australia	GmbH
q.v.	quod vide	diesbezüglich siehe
rd (3rd)	third	dritter/-e/-es
recd.	received	erhalten
regd.	registered	eingeschrieben
R.O.G.	receipt of goods	Erhalt der Waren
R.P.	reply paid	Antwort bezahlt
rsvp	répondez s'il vous plaît	um Antwort wird gebeten
S/A	Statement of Account	Kontoauszug
sgd.	signed	gez., gezeichnet
Sqr.	square	Platz
SR&CC	(free from) strikes, riots and civil commotion	(Ausgeschlossen) Streik, Aufruhr und Bürgerunruhen
st (1st)	first	erster/-e/-es
th (4th)	fourth	vierter/-e/-es usw.
Through B/L, Thru B/L	through bill of lading	Durchkonnossement
T.T.	telegraphic transfer	telegraphische Überweisung
v.	vide	siehe
VAT	value added tax	Mehrwertsteuer
W(P)A	with (particular) average	Teilschaden ist mitversichert
WB, w/b	waybill (AE)	waybill
wt.	weight	Gewicht
yd.	yard	yard

Verzeichnis wichtiger Organisationen

BSI	British Standards Institution	Britischer Normenausschuß
BT	British Telecom	Britische Fernmeldegesellschaft
CBI	Confederation of British Industry	Britischer Arbeitgeberverband
EC	European Community	Europäische Gemeinschaft
EEA	European Economic Area	Europäischer Wirtschaftsraum
EEC	European Economic Community	Europäische Wirtschaftsgemeinschaft
EFTA	European Free Trade Association	Europäische Freihandelsgemeinschaft
EIB	European Investment Bank	Europäische Investitionsbank
ERP	European Recovery Programme	Europäisches Wiederaufbauprogramm
ETUC	European Trade Union Confederation	Europäischer Gewerkschaftsbund
EU	European Union	Europäische Union
GATT	General Agreement on Tariffs and Trade	Allgemeines Zoll- und Handelsabkommen
GPO	General Post Office	Britische Post
IATA	International Air Transport Association	Internationaler Luftverkehrsverband
IBCC	International Bureau of Chambers of Commerce	Internationales Büro der Handelskammern
IBRD	International Bank for Reconstruction and Development	Internationale Bank für Wiederaufbau und Entwicklung
ICAO	International Civil Aviation Organisation	Internationale Zivilluftfahrtsorganisation
ICC	International Chamber of Commerce	Internationale Handelskammer
IEA	International Energy Agency	Internationale Energieagentur
IMF	International Monetary Fund	Internationaler Währungsfonds
ISO	International Standards Organisation	Internationale Standardorganisation

MOT (test)	Ministry of Transport (Test)	Kraftfahrzeugüberwachungsamt (TÜV-Abnahme)
NAFTA	North American Free Trade Agreement	Nordamerikanisches Freihandelsabkommen
NATO	North Atlantic Treaty Organisation	Organisation des Nordatlantikpaktes
NCM-UK	NCM Credit Insurance Limited	Nachfolgerin der Versiche rungsgruppe ECGD (Export Credit Guarantee Department) der brit. Regierung. Entspricht der deutschen Ausfuhrkreditversicherungsanstalt HERMES
OECD	Organisation for Economic Co-operation and Development	Organisation für wirtschaftliche Zusammenarbeit und Entwicklung
OPEC	Organisation of Petroleum Exporting Countries	Organisation Erdöl exportierender Länder
SITPRO	Simplification of International Trade Procedures Board	Behörde für die Vereinfachung internationaler Handelsverfahren
SWIFT	Society for Worldwide Interbank Financial Telecommunication	Gesellschaft für den internationalen Zahlungsverkehr zwischen Banken mittels Datenfernübertragung
TUC	Trades Union Congress	Britischer Gewerkschaftsbund
UNCED	United Nations Conference on Environment and Development	Umwelt- und Entwicklungskonferenz der Vereinigten Nationen
UNCTAD	United Nations Conference on Trade and Development	Welthandels- und Entwicklungskonferenz der Vereinten Nationen
UNIDO	United Nations Industrial Development Organisation	Organisation der Vereinten Nationen für industrielle Entwicklung

Briefmuster und Briefumschläge im Original-Layout

1. Blockform

LANCASHIRE
ENTERPRISES plc

Enterprise House
17 Ribblesdale Place · Winckley Square
Preston PR1 3NA
Tel: (0772) 203020 · Fax (0772) 204129
Telex: 67257 LANENT G

Your ref.: JB/lf
Our ref.: Pa. 143.421

14 March 1994

Mr Johannes Becker
Europlastik GmbH
Postweg 7
D-82178 Puchheim
Germany

Dear Mr Becker

Your enquiry of 2 March 1994

Thank you very much for your recent enquiry about our products and those of the firms we represent. We enclose our current catalogue and price lists, together with our terms of delivery. Discounts are, of course, dependent on the size of the order submitted.

We would be only too happy to send you samples of specific products, subject to certain conditions, or to arrange for a representative to visit you and help you to define your needs more closely. If you have any questions, please do not hesitate to contact me or our Sales Manager, Annette Mason, at the telephone number above. We look forward to hearing from you shortly.

Yours sincerely
Lancashire Enterprises plc

J. L. Palmerstone

J. L. Palmerstone
Managing Director

Enc

cc: Annette Mason, Sales Dept.

Lancashire House
Watery Lane
Preston PR2 2XE
Tel.: (0772) 203020
Fax (0772) 721029

Registered office:
Enterprise House · 17 Ribblesdale Place
Winckley Square · Preston PR1 3NA
Registered in England and Wales No: 2401383
A member of IMRO

Lancaster House
36 rue Breydel
1040 Brussels
Belgium
Tel: 32 2 230 34 38

2. Amerikanischer Brief in Blockform mit Zeichensetzung in Anrede und Schlußformel

The InterStay Hotel

1114 Seventh Avenue
New York
NY 1033
phone 212 383 4621
fax 212 383 4678

April 20, 1994

Mr. Wolfgang Zimmermann
Schulz Import- und Export mbH
Kurfürstenstr. 20
90459 Nürnberg
Germany

Dear Mr. Zimmermann:

This letter confirms your reservation for a double room with bath for July 16–20.

We have also reserved our conference facilities in the Manhattan Suite for your exclusive use on July 19 until 11 P.M. The room seats up to 15 people comfortably and will satisfy your needs for a small, but intensive one-day conference. We enclose our information material which, we hope, will answer your remaining questions.

Please let us know your further requirements, for example, as regards support facilities (video, tape recorders, etc.) as soon as possible. May we also ask you to request your conference guests who would like to book their own rooms in the hotel to contact us at an early date.

Sincerely yours,
The InterStay Hotel

Samuel B. Long

Samuel B. Long
General Manager

Enclosures

3. Eingerückte Form mit Zeichensetzung

Southall Groceries

42 Clarence Parade
Southall
Middlessex
MX3 6ZZ
Tel. 081249 5462

14th February, 1994

The Hackney Trading Company Ltd.,
120 –124 Canal Road,
LONDON NW3 6GH.

Dear Sirs,

Thank you for your letter of February 1st in which you inform us that your company is to cease trading due to the early retirement of Mr Newbury. We were saddened by the news as you have been a reliable trading partner over the last few years. May we take this opportunity of wishing Mr Newbury all the very best for his retirement.

We shall be placing a further large order with you before the deadline for orders expires on March 31st. We should be grateful, however, if you could recommend in due course a firm which can supply us to your own high standards after this date.

Yours faithfully,

Terence Jones

Terence Jones
Proprietor.

4. Briefumschlag mit Anschrift in Großbritannien

LANCASHIRE
ENTERPRISES plc

Enterprise House
17 Ribblesdale Place · Winckley Square
Preston PR1 3NA

Seaboard Industries Plc
Grand Avenue
Hove
East Sussex
BN3 2LS

5. Briefumschlag mit Anschrift in den Vereinigten Staaten

The InterStay Hotel

1114 Seventh Avenue
New York
NY 1033

MR JOHN D ENRIGHT
COMPUTRONIC INC
PO BOX 8732
AUSTIN TX 75110

Alphabetisches Sachregister

Die Tilde ~ steht für das halbfette Stichwort. Die Ziffern geben die Nummer des Briefes an.